Rechtsvergleichung und Rechtsvereinheitlichung

herausgegeben von der

Gesellschaft für Rechtsvergleichung e. V.

107

Model EU and Pattern OHADA?

Perspectives of a Mutual Influence in Commercial Law

Edited by

Peter Jung

Mohr Siebeck

Peter Jung, born in 1965; Professor of Private Law at the University of Basel.

ISBN 978-3-16-200020-0 / eISBN 978-3-16-200128-3
DOI 10.1628/978-3-16-200128-3

ISSN 1861-5449 / eISSN 2569-426X (Rechtsvergleichung und Rechtsvereinheitlichung)

The Deutsche Nationalbibliothek lists this publication in the Deutsche Nationalbibliographie; detailed bibliographic data are available at *https://dnb.dnb.de*.

Printed on non-aging paper. Typesetting: Laupp & Göbel, Gomaringen

Mohr Siebeck GmbH & Co. KG, Wilhelmstraße 18, 72074 Tübingen, Germany
www.mohrsiebeck.com, info@mohrsiebeck.com

Preface

The 39th conference of the German Society for Comparative Law was held from 12th to 14th September 2024 in Berlin under the general theme "Global South – Global North". This volume contains all the papers presented at the working session of the Section for Comparative Commercial and Business Law on the topic "Model EU and Pattern OHADA? – Perspectives of a Mutual Influence in Commercial Law". 140 years after the beginning of the so-called Berlin Conference concerning the Scramble for Africa, which formed a key event in the sinister history of colonisation, this comparative approach also reflects the paradigm shift in the relationship between Europe and Africa.

Today, the European Union (EU) and the Organisation pour l'harmonisation en Afrique du droit des affaires (OHADA) are the two most integrated supranational organisations in the world. On the one hand, OHADA was institutionally modelled on the EU. The association of Benin, Burkina Faso, Cameroon, the Central African Republic, Chad, Comoros, the Republic of Congo, the Democratic Republic of Congo, Côte d'Ivoire, Equatorial Guinea, Gabon, Guinea, Guinea-Bissau, Mali, Niger, Senegal, and Togo is governed by the Conference of Heads of State and Government, the Council of Ministers (Yaundé), the Common Court of Justice and Arbitration (Abidjan) and the Permanent Secretariat (Yaundé). On the other hand, the African organisation is more focused on the unification of business law across its Member States than on the establishment of a single market, to which the OHADA Treaty, unlike the TEU and TFEU, makes no reference. Based on an essentially French legal tradition, OHADA was able to go much further in the unification of commercial law, as evidenced by meanwhile eleven Uniform Acts relating to principally all aspects of general commercial, company, accounting, securities, insolvency and execution law, as well as arbitration and mediation. There are also two preliminary drafts on contract and labour law.

Against this background, the first question that arises is how much and which uniform law the players in a uniform market need and how this standardised law can be achieved. This question, which is currently being raised in the European Union in connection with the project for a European Business Code, will be addressed by *Matthias Lehmann* (Vienna). The history of OHADA as well as the institutional and legal-cultural conditions of legal harmonisation and unification in both economic areas will then be examined by *Paul Bayzelon* (Paris), who had the opportunity to participate, alongside African governments, in the implementation of OHADA in the early nineties. *Gérard Anou* (Grenoble) takes a closer look at the two key Uniform Acts relating to general commercial law and to commercial companies' law, and compares these acts with respective secondary law of the European Union. As OHADA is, apart from the English-speaking part of Cameroon, an association of former Belgian, French, German, Portuguese and Spanish colonies, it will be interesting to see whether the unification of business law can also be extended in the future to countries that have not been influenced by Civil Law. In this respect, the contribution of *Seyoum Yohannes Tesfay* (Addis Ababa/Berlin) deals with the influence of OHADA's Uniform Act relating to General Commercial Law on the Revised Commercial Code of Ethiopia. Considering that the Common Court of Justice and Arbitration also acts as a court of final appeal principally on all matters relating to the OHADA-Treaty or the Uniform Acts and that OHADA adopted Uniform Acts on arbitration and mediation in commercial matters, *Nestor Kouami* (Paris) looks at the legal framework for the judicial and alternative settlement of commercial disputes in OHADA and EU areas following a comparative approach. Finally, *Jean-Jacques Lecat* (Paris) presents a comparative analysis of commercial activity in the two supranational legal systems from the companies' point of view.

I would like to thank the speakers for their participation in the conference and for the publication of their contributions in this volume. I am also indebted to Mr David Ballmer for the linguistic review of the text, as well as Ms Esther Jundt and Ms Maria Schneider for their help with the printing. Ms. Paula Blank supported me as secretary of the working group in preparing the conference, for which I would also like to thank her warmly.

Basel, July 2025 *Peter Jung*

Table of contents

From OHADA to the EU: How much uniform law is needed for a single market?

Matthias Lehmann

I. Introducing and Delineating the Topic

The European Union (EU) is a peculiar animal. Its core aim remains the single market, yet its private law rules are still scattered over 27 different Member States' legal systems. Throughout the history of the EU and its predecessors – the European Economic Community (EEC) and the European Community (EC) – the debate over the need for private law harmonisation or unification frequently flared up. While it has calmed down nowadays, it has never completely ceased[1]. The need for private law unification is currently discussed in the areas of insolvency and capital markets, whereas in the past, other subjects have taken centre stage, such as corporate law or contract law. The debate seems dictated by the unpredictability of current events and political circumstances. A guiding rod is missing. This contribution seeks to fill this gap. It aims to clarify, at a theoretical level, how much uniform law is needed by giving reasons that are independent of time, place, and political preferences.

From the outset, some terminological clarification is in order. The term "uniform law" is used here in the sense of a rule applying throughout the market. Uniform law needs to be distinguished from "harmonised law". Harmonised law is national law that is similar but differing in detail as a result of the national legislator's discretion of. A paradigm example of uniform law is an EU regulation[2], whereas a typical example of harmonised law is a national statute transposing an EU directive.

---

[1] Among recent publications on the subject, see e.g. *Francisco de Elizalde* (ed.), Uniform Rules for European Contract Law?: A Critical Assessment (Hart Publishing 2020); *Paula Giliker*, Research Handbook on EU Tort Law (Edward Elgar Publishing 2017); *André Janssen, Matthias Lehmann and Reiner Schulze*, The Future of European Private Law (Nomos 2023).

[2] A caveat must be made here. Recently, there has been a tendency of the EU legislator to leave certain issues within the scope of a regulation to the national legislator. An illustration is Article 35a of the Regulation on credit rating agencies (Regulation [EC] No 1060/2009 of the European Parliament and of the Council of 16th September 2009 on credit rating agencies, [2009] OJ L 302/1, as amended by Regulation [EU] 462/2013 of the European Parliament and of the Council of 21st May 2013, [2013] OJ L 16/1), providing for a civil liability regime, but leaving the definition of important notions such as "damage", "intention" or "gross negli-

This contribution focuses on commercial law or, as it is sometimes called, business law. The reason for this focus is the vital role that this area plays in establishing a single market. Roy Goode, a master of the subject, has defined commercial law as

> "that body of law which governs commercial transactions, that is, agreements and arrangements between professionals for the provision and acquisition of goods, services and facilities in the way of trade."[3]

In his view, commercial law possesses four characteristics. First, it is based on transactions, not institutions; second, it is concerned primarily with dealings between merchants; third, it is centred on contracts and on the usages of the market; and fourth, it is concerned with a large mass of transactions in which each participant is a regular player[4]. The concept of business law is somewhat broader. In addition to commercial law rules, it also covers corporate law (business organisation) and other areas, such as intellectual property law. Over the course of this contribution, the essential elements of both commercial and business law will become clearer.

A further terminological clarification is necessary. When the expression "single market" is used in the following, what is meant is any market in which products (goods and services) as well as production factors (workers and capital) can move freely and independently of the participating state from which they originate. The concept of the single market underlying this contribution is thus identical to that of a "common market" that prevailed before the Single European Act in 1986, which introduced the term "internal market"; the change in terminology seems to have been induced by political considerations and not by a conceptual distinction[5]. A single, common or internal market must however be distinguished from a "free-trade zone", which is characterised by an abolition of customs between the members, as well as from a "customs union", which entails unified customs duties with regard to non-members[6]. Free-trade zones and customs unions do not necessarily require legal unification or even harmonisation of rules other than those concerning customs.

Finally, a further delineation is necessary. This contribution focuses on uniform *private* law rules, particularly commercial or business law. Regulatory

---

gence" to the national legislator, see Article 35a(4). This can hardly qualify as uniform law. Moreover, it also seems to be contrary to the purpose and function of a regulation, as defined by Article 288(3) Treaty on the Functioning of the European Union (TFEU).

[3] *Roy Goode*, 'The Codification of Commercial Law', (1988) 14 Monash University Law Review 135, 141.

[4] Ibid.

[5] See *Pierre Pescatore*, 'Some Critical Remarks on the Single European Act', (1987) 24 Common Market Law Review 11 (criticising the notion "Internal Market" for being one-sided and based on an arbitrary selection of the Treaty objectives).

[6] On free-trade zones and customs unions see Article XXIV General Agreement on Tariffs and Trade (GATT).

rules will only occasionally be touched upon. Of course, there can be no doubt that the unification of regulatory rules, in subjects such as competition, health and safety standards, or marketing requirements, is vital for the emergence and the functioning of a single market. It is left out in this contribution merely because the EU has already made great progress in enacting uniform rules in this regard. The same cannot be said of private law, where the diversity of Member States' laws still reigns. The question posed here concerns the extent to which this diversity endangers the proper functioning of the single market.

The remainder of this contribution is divided into two parts. The first will take stock of experiences made in other parts of the world, both geographically (by comparing existing modern legal systems) and historically (by comparing ancient legal systems). The second part will then provide analytical reasons when and why uniform laws are required for market integration.

II. Empirical Data: Comparisons in Space and Time

1. Single Markets and Private Law in the World Today

Looking around the world, one can observe that states aiming to integrate their economies typically resort to uniform commercial law. A striking example is the Organisation for the Harmonisation of Commercial Law in Africa (*Organisation pour l'Harmonisation en Afrique du Droit des Affaires* – OHADA), which has produced various uniform law acts. OHADA's most significant achievement to date is the Act on General Commercial Law[7]. It deals with all subjects one would expect in a national codification of commercial law. Among others, it includes rules on the status of the merchant and the entrepreneur; the commercial register; commercial leases; the transfer of business; intermediaries, such as brokers and agents; and sales contracts. Besides the Act on General Commercial Law, there are also uniform acts on company law and business interest groups, cooperatives, accounting law and financial information, carriage of goods by road, and secured transactions[8]. Even the law of enforcement and insolvency has been unified[9].

---

[7] OHADA, Acte uniforme du 15 décembre 2010 portant sur le droit commercial général.

[8] OHADA, Acte uniforme révisé du 30 janvier 2014 relatif au droit des sociétés commerciales et du groupement d'intérêt économique; Acte uniforme du 15 janvier 2010 relatif au droit des sociétés coopératives; Acte uniforme du 26 janvier 2017 relatif au droit comptable et à l'information financière; Acte uniforme du 22 mars 2003 relatif aux contrats de transport de marchandises par route; Acte uniforme révisé du 15 décembre 2010 portant organisation des sûretés.

[9] OHADA, Acte uniforme du 17 octobre 2023 portant organisation des procédures simplifiées de recouvrement et des voies d'exécution; Acte uniforme du 10 septembre 2015 portant organisation des procédures collectives d'apurement du passif.

Comparably high degrees of unification of commercial law can be found in other jurisdictions. One example is Spain. While the Autonomous Communities (*Comunidades autónomas*) may set idiosyncratic private law rules, commercial law is entirely unified. The Commercial Code (*Código de comercio*) applies throughout the whole country. The underlying intention seems to be the avoidance of obstacles to trade and commerce between the different Spanish regions.

A further example is India, where different versions of the Common law apply throughout the 28 states and eight territories. To prevent this legal diversity from impeding trade, the federal legislator has unified a vast number of legal rules. Among them are those on contract law, negotiable instruments, trusts, cooperatives, corporate law, labour law, copyright, trademarks, and competition law[10].

These three examples are textbook models of commercial law unification. Their maximalist positions are not supported by everyone. Sceptics of uniform law will highlight the benefits of legal diversity, such as regulatory competition, the policy space of governments, or democratic self-determination. To cite just one example, many integrated markets, such as the US, do not have uniform rules on corporate law. However, this does not seem to create problems. On the contrary, the existence of different corporate laws creates the conditions of a laboratory in which the "best", "optimal", and "most efficient" rules will eventually prevail[11]. This healthy kind of competition is lost through uniform law.

There are also instances where the degree of commercial law unification is more limited. In the absence of a comprehensive federal power to regulate private law issues, the federal states of the US have voluntarily coordinated their business law – except corporate law – through the activities of the Uniform Law Commission[12]. The Commission is mainly active in the area of trade and commerce, with its most successful text being the Uniform Commercial Code (UCC). Currently, the UCC contains rules on sales and lease contracts, nego-

---

[10] See Indian Contract Act 1872; Negotiable Instruments Act 1881; Trusts Act 1882; Cooperative Societies Act 1912; Trade Unions Act, 1926; Industrial Employment (Standing Orders) Act 1946; Industrial Disputes Act 1947; Minimum Wages Act 1948; Companies Act 1956; Copyright Act 1957; Trade Marks Act 1999; Competition Act 2002; Multi State Co-Operative Societies Act 2002. These acts are reprinted in *Germano Franceschin and Francesco Misuraca*, India: Commercial, Customs and Tax Law (Wolters Kluwer 2011), Appendices.

[11] *Ralph K. Winter*, 'State Law, Shareholder Protection, and the Theory of the Corporation', (1977) 6 The Journal of Legal Studies 251, 254–258 (rejecting the "race to the bottom" theory according to which competition between state corporate laws would promote the law with the lowest standard of investor protection); *Frank H. Easterbrook and Daniel R. Fischel*, The Economic Structure of Corporate Law (Harvard University Press 1996) 213–216 (discussing the force of competition between states for incorporations); *Roberta Romano*, 'The States as a Laboratory: Legal Innovation and State Competition for Corporate Charters', (2006) 23 Yale Journal on Regulation 209 (showing how formulations tested successfully in one state are taken over by the vast majority of other states).

[12] Official title: National Conference of Commissioners on Uniform State Laws.

tiable instruments, bank deposits and collections, funds transfers, letters of credit, bulk sales, documents of title, investment securities, secured transactions, and controllable electronic records[13]. In comparison with the uniform acts of OHADA, this is only a fraction. Nevertheless, it seems that interstate commerce in the US is functioning reasonably well, which may be primarily due to the similarities of the Common law in general.

More examples of markets with partially uniform laws exist around the world. Canada, whose provinces variously follow the Common law or the Civil law tradition, has federalised the law on the sale of goods, bills of exchange, and personal property; the Uniform Law Conference of Canada (ULCC) has added an act on securities transfers[14]. Australia, despite having differentiated private law, has also federalised some parts of commercial law, in particular the sale of goods and personal property securities, in addition to consumer law[15]. The United Kingdom, which comprises three systems of private law (English law, Scots law, and the law of Northern Ireland), has enacted statutes that apply throughout the whole country, in particular in the area of bills of exchange and the sale of goods[16].

A differentiated picture presents itself from this brief overview. Legal unification seems to be an essential pillar of market integration. This is particularly true for rules that are traditionally considered to be part of commercial law. Among the rules of commercial law that have been unified, the rules on the sale of goods and negotiable instruments, including securities, stand out. Even those states that do not dispose of a common private law have at least unified these rules. This has happened irrespective of whether there was a federal power for unification or not. Even those states whose constitution does not provide for such a power have unified their rules through voluntary coordination of the provinces or federal states.

2. *Comparisons in Time*

The preceding analysis of existing legal systems provides strong indications for a correlation between integrated markets and uniform legal rules. However, correlation must not be confused with causation. Even if there were causation, it remains unclear in which direction it operated, i. e. what was first: market in-

[13] See the website of the ULC: https://www.uniformlaws.org/acts/overview (last visited on 10th July 2025).

[14] See Sale of Goods Act 1978, Bills of Exchange Act 1985; Personal Property Act 1993, and Securities Transfer Act 2007. For context, see *Roderick J. Wood*, 'The Codification of Commercial Law', (2016) 79 Saskatchewan Law Review 179, 180–181 (mentioning that the first two go back to the English tradition, whereas the last two were heavily influenced by the US).

[15] See *Dilan Thampapillai and others*, Australian Commercial Law (Cambridge University Press 2020).

[16] See Bills of Exchange Act 1882; Sale of Goods Act 1979.

tegration or unification of commercial law. This hen-and-egg problem can most convincingly be overcome by a historical analysis. By going back in time, it can be shown that the introduction of uniform rules of commercial law typically preceded the emergence of common or single markets, and not the other way around.

Our journey starts in France at the end of the 17th Century. King Louis XIV's influential and energetic First Minister of State, Jean-Baptiste Colbert, brought forward two decrees on commerce on land and commerce on sea[17]. These acts laid the groundwork for trade within France and with other countries, at a time when the rest of French private law was still fragmented[18]. They set models not only for France but also for the rest of the world and were widely admired[19]. Their provisions were used as a basis for the French Commercial Code promulgated in 1807, three years after the French Civil Code. They were instrumental in paving the way for the strong national economy.

The next stop on our historical journey is Germany, which had been split up after the Napoleonic Wars, aggravating its fragmentation of private law systems until the adoption of a Civil Code in 1896. But commercial unification had commenced long before this date, even before the German unification of 1871. As early as 1861, the General Assembly of the German Confederation had suggested a "General German Commercial Code" (*Allgemeines Deutsches Handelsgesetzbuch* – ADHGB)[20]. It was implemented by many member states, such as Prussia, Bavaria, and Austria. Before that, a General Act on Bills of Exchange had been adopted in 1848 by the short-lived National Assembly in Frankfurt

---

[17] Ordonnance sur le commerce de terre (1673) (also known as the "Code Savary"); Ordonnance sur le commerce de mer (1681) (also known as "Ordonnance sur la marine"). On these acts, see *Yves Guyon*, Droit des affaires, vol. 1, 8th ed. (LGDJ 1994) 16; *Joël Monéger*, 'De l'Ordonnance de Colbert de 1673 sur le commerce au Code de commerce français de septembre 2000: Réflexion sur l'aptitude du droit économique et commercial à la codification', (2004) 18 Revue internationale de droit économique 171, 175–176.

[18] Before the French Revolution, French law was fragmented between the North, where around 60 customary laws and more than 360 different local or particular laws applied, and the South, where Roman law applied as "written law" (*droit écrit*). See *Jacques Poumarède*, 'De la fin des coutumes à la survie des usages locaux – Le Code civil face aux particularismes', (2009) 1 Histoire de la Justice 173, 174.

[19] See *Roger Houin*, 'Reform of the French Civil Code and the Code of Commerce', (1955) 4 The American Journal of Comparative Law 485 (commending the 'lucidity and precision of the style' of the codes and calling them 'monuments of law'); in a similar vein *Jean Chadelat*, 'L'élaboration de l'Ordonnance de la marine d'août 1681', (1954) 31 Revue historique de droit français et étranger 74 (highlighting the quality of style, expression and composition of the decree on commerce by sea). For a critical appraisal, see *Monéger* (n. 17) 178 (stating that the Code Savary contained nothing new).

[20] On the history and content, see *Ralf Heimann*, Die Entwicklung der handelsrechtlichen Veröffentlichung vom ALR bis zum ADHGB (Duncker & Humblot 2008) 236 et seq."plainCitation":"On the history and content, see Ralf Heimann, Die Entwicklung der handelsrechtlichen Veröffentlichung vom ALR bis zum ADHGB. (1. Auflage, Duncker & Humblot GmbH 2008

and enacted in individual states[21]. The objective of these codifications was to facilitate trade and cross-border commerce in the German-speaking parts of the former Holy Roman Empire, in a bid to increase the wealth of the participating states. They led to the emergence of a common market and closer integration. In the long run, this paved the way for political unification.

Remarkably, commercial law unification preceded economic and political integration in France and Germany, the two biggest EU member states. One may even go further back in time, to the Roman Empire, to witness the same phenomenon. The Romans did of course not adopt formal codifications of commercial law, as they were less interested in trading than in *consuming* the riches others had produced[22]. But to be able to do so, it was in their interest to stimulate trade among the provinces, and between the provinces and Rome. In this context, it is important to remember that Roman law consisted of two different sets of rules: the *ius civile* for relations between Roman citizens and the *ius gentium* for relations between non-Romans as well as between Romans and non-Romans[23]. The *ius gentium* was developed by a special judge, the *praetor peregrinus*, who had jurisdiction over disputes involving foreigners[24]. This judge did not have any knowledge of foreign laws, nor the intention to investigate them. In the absence of applicable rules, he developed new substantive rules *ad hoc*[25]. These were rules for multi-state disputes that provided the necessary clarity and legal certainty so that commercial relationships could flourish. This body of law was later gradually incorporated into the *ius civile* and eventually codified by Emperor Justinian in the Digest[26]. In this way, Roman civil law took over all the institutions, principles, and rules that fostered trade in the Empire for commercial relations with or without foreigners. It is probably no coincidence that it became the basis for the *ius commune*, which later governed medieval Europe and on which many continental legal systems are built to this day.

---

[21] On the Allgemeine Deutsche Wechselordnung, see *Manley O. Hudson and A. H. Feller*, 'The International Unification of Laws concerning Bills of Exchange', (1931) 44 Harvard Law Review 333, 343.

[22] *Layton B. Register*, 'Notes on the History of Commerce and Commercial Law. 1. Antiquity' (1913) 61 University of Pennsylvania Law Review and American Law Register 431, 434 (stressing that 'While the provinces produced, Rome consumed. Her commerce was one of importation.').

[23] For a certain time, there existed also a third set of rules, the *ius Latii*, for those living in Latium and in the colonies. The *ius Latii* disappeared when the Latins were made Roman citizens in about 150 AD. See *Andrew D. E. Lewis*, 'Ius Latii', Oxford Classical Dictionary (Oxford University Press 2015).

[24] *Register* (n. 22) 436 (dating the appointment of the first *praetor peregrinus* back to the 512th year after the foundation of Rome); *Symeon Symeonides*, Choice of Law (Oxford University Press 2016) 46 (stating that the *praetor peregrinus* had jurisdiction over 'disputes with foreign elements, or at least between non-Roman citizens').

[25] *Symeonides* (n. 24) 47.

[26] *Register* (n. 22) 436 (mentioning the role of the "Perpetual Edict" in this context); *Symeonides* (n. 24) 47.

3. Intermediate Conclusion

The upshot of the comparison in space and time is clear: the adoption of uniform rules governing commerce and trade typically precedes market integration. This is true both in modern laws and historically.

It is therefore all the more astonishing that the EU is not heeding the lessons lying right on its doorstep. It still thinks that it can "muddle through" with a variety of different Member State laws, which govern not only politically divisive areas such as family law and succession, but also commercial relations.

Critics may still be unconvinced. They may see the developments in other parts of the world and in Europe itself as pure coincidence. These developments, they could argue, do not demonstrate the impossibility of a different way, the "EU way". They can support their view by pointing to the fact that the areas which have been unified vary from country to country and from time to time. This raises an important question: Is it really necessary to go for complete unification, or is it sufficient to unify just some areas of the law, and if so, which? This question cannot be answered empirically, but requires a thorough theoretical analysis.

III. Theoretical Analysis

1. Economics as the Benchmark

The comparative overview above has given no clear answer to the question of *how much* unification of the law is needed for a single market. Some single markets have been shown to feature a fully-fledged, comprehensive commercial law (OHADA and Spain being examples in point). Others limit themselves to some selective rules (the US, Canada, and Australia). Neither of the two types proves which rules are essential. Instead, we need a benchmark, which must be objective and neutral. Given that the unit of analysis is a market, it seems appropriate to use economics for this purpose. In particular, the economic analysis of the law provides a rich variety of arguments and criteria that can be used to evaluate the need for uniform law. Among them are, for instance, the benefits of limiting transaction costs to the strictly necessary and the opportunities arising through economies of scale.

So far, those who have analysed the need for uniform law from an economic viewpoint have come to negative conclusions[27]. They stress the foregone bene-

[27] See e.g. *Larry E. Ribstein and Bruce H. Kobayashi*, 'An Economic Analysis of Uniform State Laws', (1996) 25 The Journal of Legal Studies 131; *Anthony Ogus*, 'Competition Between National Legal Systems: A Contribution of Economic Analysis To Comparative Law', (1999) 48 International & Comparative Law Quarterly 405; specifically for the European context

fits of regulatory competition as well as the problems and the costs of enacting uniform rules[28]. These studies concern the market in general or some particular broad field, such as corporate law, where uniformity is less beneficial. However, they have not explored the areas in which uniform rules are indispensable or produce higher benefits than diverse national rules.

2. *Secure Identification of the Applicable Law*

One should not overestimate the need for uniform law. National law is not necessarily an obstacle to free trade. Where the applicable national law can be identified with certainty through clear and straightforward conflict-of-laws rules, individuals can adapt their behaviour accordingly. Modern conflict-of-laws rules allow parties to choose, among all legal systems, the one fitting their needs best, and to structure their relation around it. Free choice of law, or "party autonomy", is a hallmark of modern conflict of laws and is recognised around the world[29]. Party autonomy provides both individual freedom and legal certainty. It also guarantees that the most beneficial legal systems will be promoted over time, in the sense of regulatory competition that economists prefer.

Surprisingly, free choice of law also has a unifying effect. A national law which parties agree on repeatedly will over time become a standard. Examples are English law and New York law in areas such as financial, insurance, or maritime law. French and Swiss law enjoy a similar status in international commercial arbitration. Despite being national laws, these legal systems are well-known internationally. This lowers information and transaction costs.

Thus, a major hypothesis for our inquiry is this: where the national law is certain or parties can choose a certain law and effectively coalesce around a specific legal system, uniform law is not needed, or at least less needed than in other areas where such freedom does not exist, or parties find it difficult to agree on a specific law. It is time to test this proposition in a few areas.

Frank H. Easterbrook, 'Federalism and European Business Law', (1994) 14 International Review of Law and Economics 125.

[28] See *Ribstein and Kobayashi* (n. 27) 135–137 (taking the view that jurisdictional competition may produce more efficient results than uniform state laws and highlighting the danger of unequal implementation); *Ogus* (n. 27) 415–416 (stressing that the benefits of uniform law may be outweighed by the costs of formulating uniform principles, reaching agreement on them, and subsequently adapting national legal systems to them); *Easterbrook* (n. 27) 131 (underscoring the benefits of diverse corporate laws).

[29] *Russell J. Weintraub*, 'Functional developments in choice of law for contracts', (1984) 187 Collection of Courses at the Academy of International Law 239, 271 (calling party autonomy 'perhaps the most widely accepted private international rule of our time').

3. Third-party Effects

From what has been said before, it follows that the need for uniform rules is greatest where the applicable law is unclear and the parties cannot overcome this uncertainty by choosing the applicable law. A salient case is where third parties are involved. A choice of the parties typically does not have any effect on those who did not acquiesce to it, according to the old Roman adage "*res inter alios acta, aliis neque nocere neque prodesse potest*"[30]. At the same time, it would be impossible to contract with all those potentially affected and agree on a single law. Not only would the transaction costs be prohibitively high, but some third parties that need to be bound by the choice may be unknown in advance. Hence, wherever such third-party effects are intended, uniform law is necessary to secure them.

Third-party effects are indispensable in the law of negotiable instruments, such as bills of exchange and cheques. These essential tools for cross-border commerce would not function without their effects on third parties. For instance, the transfer of the claim embodied in the instrument purports to have effects against third parties, such as the drawee, creditors, or insolvency administrators, no matter where they live or are established. This effect must be guaranteed by every state in which negotiable instruments are used. Also, negotiable instruments create liabilities towards future third parties: those who accept them are liable to any future holder. Again, this effect must work independently of the domicile or location of the third party.

Against this backdrop, it is hardly surprising that the law of negotiable instruments was an early case of private law unification. Whenever common markets were created, uniform rules on negotiable instruments were the first to be introduced[31]. Two of the first conventions on uniform law, concluded in the 1930s, aimed at creating worldwide uniform rules for bills of exchange and cheques[32]. This target was missed because Common law countries abstained from signing these conventions. Still, the ratification by many Civil law countries demonstrates a conviction that uniform rules on negotiable instruments are indispensable for trade.

Cheques and bills of exchange are today somewhat dated. But similar problems also arise in relation to securities, like shares or bonds. Their transfer is designed to produce effects against third parties. The acquirer of a share will

---

[30] See *Manuel C. Firic*[illegible], 'The Concept of the Principle of Relativity of the Effects of the Contract: Regulation and Foundation', (2020) 6 Journal of Law and Public Administration 119.

[31] See Allgemeine Deutsche Wechselordnung supra II. 2; Article 3 UCC; the Australian and Canadian Bills of Exchange Acts supra II. 1; Indian Negotiable Instruments Act 1881.

[32] See Convention providing a Uniform Law for Bills of Exchange and Promissory Notes, done in Geneva on 7th June 1930; Convention providing a Uniform Law for Cheques, done in Geneva on 19th March 1931.

become a member of the issuing company in relation to the other shareholders and the whole world, and the acquirer of a bond becomes the creditor of the claim embodied in the bond in relation to the debtor and the whole world. Determining the applicable law to these intended third-party effects is difficult[33]. This may explain why many states with integrated markets have adopted uniform rules on them[34].

Third-party effects must also be guaranteed in secured transactions, in which collateral and other security rights are granted. This need is most conspicuous with regard to movables because they may cross borders. Undoubtedly for this reason, Australia and Canada have federalised the law of personal property security[35]. A similar rule for the EU would be of great help.

Third-party effects must also be secured with regard to intangible property. Determining the applicable law in this area is fraught with difficulties. An example is the assignment of claims, where the EU has tried for many years to introduce a uniform conflict-of-laws rule, so far to no avail[36]. A uniform substantive rule of law could overcome these difficulties single-handedly. Such a rule would be relatively easy to draft and would be politically acceptable because it is better than legal diversity in this area[37]. Another example of intangible property that could benefit from uniform rules are digital assets. The law applying to cryptocurrencies and other digital assets is notoriously difficult to identify. It is no coincidence that the US Uniform Law Commission suggests new rules to be added to the UCC on "controllable electronic records", aka digital assets[38].

Another area with potential third-party effects is insolvency. Efficient and fair insolvency proceedings in common markets typically require cross-border effectiveness under the principle of universality[39]. Such cross-border effectiveness can be secured by a rule of recognition[40]. However, the effectiveness of creditors' collateral rights may suffer due to diverging creditor hierarchies in Member States. Therefore, overcoming these divergences should be at the top of the legislator's agenda. Instead, the EU has focused on pre-insolvency proce-

---

[33] See *Matthias Lehmann*, 'Financial Instruments', in *Jürgen Basedow et al.* (eds.), Encyclopedia of Private International Law (Edward Elgar Publishing 2017).

[34] See e.g. Article 8 UCC on Investment Securities; Canadian Securities Transfer Act 2007.

[35] See supra II. 1.

[36] See European Commission, Proposal for a Regulation of the European Parliament and of the Council on the law applicable to the third-party effects of assignments of claims, COM (2018) 96 final.

[37] For an example what such a rule could look like, see the European Business Code Book 8 on banking law, Chapter 2 Section 1 Article 8.2.2.1.1.1. et seq (available at www.henricapitant.org/actions/draft-european-business-code; last visited on 10th July 2025).

[38] See Article 12 UCC.

[39] On the universality of insolvency proceedings, see e.g. *Gerard McCormack*, 'Universalism in Insolvency Proceedings and the Common Law', (2012) 32 Journal of Legal Studies 325.

[40] See e.g. Article 19(1) European Insolvency Regulation.

dures, especially on restructuring[41]. This may have been useful to modernise some Member States' laws, yet was not strictly required, as finding the most effective restructuring procedure could also have been left to the legislative competition of national laws. It would be much more important to focus on the insolvency hierarchy, even if this may be difficult politically.

In conclusion, uniform law is most useful where effects against third parties must be guaranteed. This effect can typically not be reached by a choice of law. Areas in point are the law of negotiable instruments, the law of securities, secured transactions, intangible assets, and insolvency. This list is by no means complete and may have to be updated in line with technological, economic and market developments.

4. Mandatory Rules

A further reason why unification may be needed is mandatory rules. Diverging mandatory rules of national law lead to a fragmentation of the legal framework of the market. Parties cannot contract around the mandatory rules but must obey a multitude of varying and perhaps even contradicting requirements.

Such mandatory rules are omnipresent in regulatory law. This is why the EU has concentrated its efforts on introducing a Union-wide regulatory framework. The four fundamental freedoms are applied principally to overcome obstacles resulting from different regulatory rules. Countless directives and regulations serve the same aim.

Yet regulatory rules may also directly interfere with private relationships. A good illustration is competition law. The prohibition of restraints of competition directly interferes with the freedom of contract. This is why it made sense to unify the prohibition at Union level[42].

The same reasoning applies to so-called overriding mandatory rules. These are binding irrespective of the law that has been chosen. Typically, they serve the common good and the public interest. Examples include the rules on liability for misleading financial information or false credit ratings, the rules on supply chains, or those on data protection and security. A choice of law in these areas is typically excluded. At the same time, they pose ardent conflict-of-laws issues. To be effective throughout the market, states may elevate some of their idiosyncratic rules to the level of overriding mandatory rules[43]. This tendency

[41] Directive (EU) 2019/1023 of the European Parliament and of the Council of 20th June 2019 on preventive restructuring frameworks, on discharge of debt and disqualifications, and on measures to increase the efficiency of procedures concerning restructuring, insolvency and discharge of debt, OJ (2019) L 172, 18.

[42] Article 101 TFEU.

[43] See the Belgian law of commercial agents. Fortunately, Belgian courts no longer consider this law to be of an overriding nature, see Cour de cassation, 12th June 2023, THIBELO v Stölzle-Oberglas, ECLI:BE:CASS:2023:ARR.20230407.1N.6.

should be fought by all means because of its destructive effect on the single market. It therefore makes sense to delimit and unify the issues that are covered by overriding mandatory rules[44].

Some mandatory rules cannot be excluded, even though they are not of an overriding mandatory nature. An example is standard terms control. While the rules on the unfairness of standard contract terms are subject to a choice of law by the parties, the same is not true for the rules determining whether a certain clause, including a choice-of-law clause, has become part of the contract, e.g. the rule protecting against surprising clauses. Since this rule concerns the very conclusion of the contract, it cannot be deselected by one of its terms. Hence, uniform law in this area is of the essence.

A tricky question concerns the liability of the acquirer of a commercial enterprise for the acquired enterprise's debt. Some Member States provide for such a liability where the enterprise is continued under the same or under a different business name [45]. Typically, the statutory liability cannot be excluded by contract between the acquirer and the seller of the enterprise[46]. Other Member States do not have a similar rule. This makes the question which law governs this liability all the more important. Opinions on this subject diverge strongly[47]. A uniform rule on this subject could provide legal certainty and strengthen the market for enterprise control.

5. Transaction Costs

Comprehensive unification of substantive commercial law, although perhaps helpful, seems unnecessary. Save for some special cases of (overriding) mandatory rules, the law governing business transactions (B2B) can be freely chosen. Party autonomy allows businesses to select, among the various national rules, those that best respond to their needs. Where they tend to agree on a specific

[44] For the proposal of a uniform EU rule on prospectus liability, see *Danny Busch and Matthias Lehmann*, 'Uniform Prospectus Liability Rules for Europe', (2023) 14 Journal of European Tort Law 113.

[45] See e.g. Section 25 German Commercial Code (HGB); Section 38 Austrian Commercial Code (UGB); Section 1409 Austrian Civil Code (ABGB); Article L141-17-22 French Commercial Code (CCom).

[46] See Article 1409(3) ABGB. Section 25(2) HGB and Section 38(4) UGB allow the exclusion of liability by publishing the agreement between the enterprise's seller and the acquirer to that effect in the commercial register (for the UGB, another generally recognized manner of publication or individual notification suffices).

[47] See, e.g., *Matthias Lehmann*, 'Die Lücke im europäischen Kollisionsrecht der Schuldverhältnisse? Die Haftung wegen Vermögensübernahme und wegen Fortführung eines Handelsgeschäfts', [2015] IPRax 495 (favouring the treatment as overriding mandatory rules); *Robert Freitag*, 'Art. 9 Rom I-VO und Art. 16 Rom II-VO als Superkollisionsnormen des Internationalen Schuldrechts? Gedanken zum Verhältnis zwischen internen und externen Lücken des EuIPR', [2016] IPRax 418 (advocating for the submission to national conflicts rules).

law, uniformity will spontaneously arise, not by the work of some international or supranational legislator, but by the commercial actors' own choice. It does not need to be stressed that this process is preferable to unification "top-down".

As a result, there is *a priori* no need to harmonise areas such as contract law. Given the wide recognition of party autonomy, the choice of the "best" or most appropriate contract law can be left to the market participants. Still, numerous national legislators have found it necessary to provide a uniform set of rules at least for one contract type, the sales contract[48]. Why is that?

Several explanations may be ventured. One is that business operators may fail to coalesce around a single law, instead selecting different ones. An operator with many customers would thus potentially have to deal with a variety of laws. This may increase information and transaction costs, making the introduction of a uniform regime advantageous.

Sales law unification can also be helpful to strengthen the common legal culture in a particular market. The use of the same rules may foster a legal community and its understanding of legal concepts and principles. These effects go far beyond any precise measurable economic effect and must not be underestimated. For example, the Convention on the International Sale of Goods (CISG) has been especially useful as a tool for legal education and mutual legal understanding, and has aided the emergence of a common terminology, even though its practical relevance is greatly reduced by its frequent deselection.

In sum, even though it is not strictly *necessary* to unify areas such as contract law where the applicable law can be chosen, it may be *beneficial* on multiple levels. While the unification of sales law or contract law more generally is not an *indispensable condition* for market integration, it may *contribute* to its functioning. There are thus different degrees of utility of uniform rules, which explains why they differ across existing common markets.

6. Role of Common Institutions

The foregoing analysis focused on the unification of substantive rules. Undoubtedly, common institutions and uniform rules of procedure can also significantly contribute to market integration. For this reason, OHADA has not only produced uniform rules, but also features common institutions, namely a secretariat, based in Yaoundé (Cameroon); a Common Court of Justice and Arbitration, seated in Abidjan (Ivory Coast); as well as a school for the judiciary, established in Porto Novo (Benin). The market integration of countries such as Spain, Germany, France, India, Australia, or Canada has also been greatly advanced by the existence of a common apex court, which has settled differences and

[48] The member states of OHADA, the US, the UK, Canada, and Australia all provide uniform rules on sales contracts, see supra II 1.

doubts on the interpretation of the uniform rules of commercial or business law. The US provides a counterexample. Although it has a two-tier court system, with parallel state and federal courts, the federal courts have no substantive jurisdiction for the interpretation of the UCC. They may however decide cases in which the UCC applies where both parties are from different states (diversity jurisdiction).

In the EU, the task to interpret uniform substantive rules is vested in the Court of Justice (CJEU). One may doubt whether the Court of Justice is adequately equipped for this task. Most of its judges are experts of public law, not private law. In addition, the Court already has to bear a heavy case load, to the point that jurisdiction for some case categories has recently been shifted to the General Court, which is, however, also dominated by experts in public law. It would certainly be useful to create a special chamber inside the CJEU for private law matters, or even a European Commercial Court[49]. An additional boost for market integration could be provided by EU commercial courts of first and second instance, which could decide e. g. in cross-border cases. There could be a second judicial tier, in parallel to national courts. The system could resemble that of the US, where federal and state courts exist side by side.

In sum, establishing common institutions plays a crucial role for uniformity in the interpretation and application of the law. However, the introduction of such courts makes sense only after the substantive law has been unified. In other words, it is a corollary of, and not a replacement for the unification of commercial law.

IV. Conclusion

This contribution has shown that markets cannot integrate without common rules of commercial law. It has also identified precise areas in which such common rules are indispensable. These are those areas where the parties cannot choose the applicable law and where it cannot be identified with ease and certainty. This is the case where (1) third parties are affected or (2) mandatory rules are dominant. Examples for the first category are rules concerning negotiable instruments, such as bills of exchange or cheques; or securities, such as shares or bonds; further rules that fall into this category are the rules on security interests or those on insolvency. As examples of the second category, one can cite competition law, the law on data protection, or the law of supply chains.

---

[49] See the proposal by *Giesela Rühl*, 'Building Competence in Commercial Law in the Member States', Study for the JURI Committee of the European Parliament, September 2018, 58–63.

The rules that have been cited here are relatively few. They should be understood as the absolute minimum, or core, of the rules that must be uniform. Undoubtedly, it is useful to unify further rules, such as those on intellectual property, sales law, or general contract law. Yet the objective of this contribution was to show which rules are indispensable for market integration. Regrettably, the EU has still failed to adopt many of even these core rules. It is therefore unsurprising that it has not succeeded in completing the project of a single market.

Conditions for legal harmonisation in the EU and OHADA

Paul Bayzelon

I. Introduction

The aim of this article is to trace the history of OHADA, French acronym for Organization for the Harmonization of Business Law in Africa, and to share the various lessons that can be drawn from the success of OHADA for our own continent. Matthias Lehmann already introduced the European Code of Business Law. It is indeed one of the leading projects recommended by Enrico Letta, the former chairman of Italy's Council of Ministers and the current chairman of the Jacques Delors Institute[1]. He submitted his report titled "Much more than a market –Empowering the single market"[2] to the European Council of Heads of States last April. The report deals with the strengthening of the internal market (Binnenmarkt). It may sound like a paradox, but we would not be discussing a European business code if OHADA had not existed. This goal of business law unification is already addressed in Article 20 of the Franco-German Treaty of Aachen / Aix la Chapelle, which was signed on 22nd January 2019.

As a former civil servant working for the French Ministry of Cooperation, I had the opportunity, in the early nineties, to play a part, alongside African governments, in the implementation of OHADA. This contribution is an expression of my belief that unification – not harmonization but indeed unification – of business and commercial laws is a powerful force for good, for unity and for peace. It is an extremely efficient tool which brings together economies, nations and their people.

---

[1] See: https://commission.europa.eu/enrico-letta_en; https://www.delorscentre.eu/de/ueber-uns/beirat/profil/person/letta (both last visited on 10th July 2025).

[2] *Enrico Letta*, 'Much more than a Market – Speed, Security, Solidarity – Empowering the Single Market to deliver a sustainable future and prosperity for all EU Citizens', March 2024, access the report at: https://dorie.ec.europa.eu/en/details/-/card/8000605 (last visited 10th July 2025).

II. The Beginnings of OHADA

OHADA is a dynamic process for the unification of business laws, company and commercial laws, including accounting law (accounting law is a very important piece of OHADA). Today, OHADA comprises 17 countries of sub-Saharan Africa, more than 300 million inhabitants: a unique process whose success is recognized worldwide.

This dynamic legal unification process is rooted in history. We all know that in 1884/1885, European countries signed the Treaty of Berlin, which put an end to the well-known "Scramble for Africa" ("Das Wettrennen um Afrika", "La course au clocher"). Sub-Saharan Africa was divided into areas of colonization with arbitrary linear borders. No consideration was given to ancient kingdoms and nascent or already existing nations.

From a legal perspective, one could say the Treaty of Berlin permanently ratified the *summa divisio* between common law and civil law in Western Africa, a legal divide very difficult to overcome. On the one hand, the English-speaking countries, based on Common Law of England and Wales; on the other hand, the Civil Law countries based on codified, civilist – some say Romano Germanic – legal systems: the former Belgian, French, German, Portuguese and Spanish (Equatorial Guinea) colonies[3].

In all these countries, the law of the colonizer was enforced with respect to companies, business and commerce. In the French colonies, the 1807 Code de commerce and the 1866 commercial companies' statute were the applicable business laws; in the Belgian Congo, Congo Léopoldville, the 1870's decrees of the sovereign King Leopold II still applied. The same in Burundi, with the 1861 *Allgemeines Deutsches Handelsgesetzbuch*, etc.

In most sub-Saharan countries, this situation went on until the years of decolonization: 1958/60 for most of them, 1975 for the former Portuguese countries.

At first, OHADA mainly applied to French speaking countries, members of the *Communauté Financière d'Afrique* with the CFA franc as a single currency. Spanish speaking Equatorial Guinea and Portuguese speaking Guinea Bissau became members of the CFA franc zone starting from the eighties[4].

For the sake of simplicity, let us focus on the French-speaking countries which are at the root of the OHADA process.

---

[3] *Salvatore Mancuso*, 'The New African Law: Beyond the Difference Between Common Law and Civil Law', Annual Survey of International & Comparative Law 14/1 (2008), 39, 42 and 45; *Richard Waller*, 'Legal History and Historiography in Colonial Sub-Saharan Africa', Oxford Research Encyclopedia of African History (2018), access at: https://oxfordre.com/africanhistory/view/10.1093/acrefore/9780190277734.001.0001/acrefore-9780190277734-e-548 (last visited on 10th July 2025).

[4] *Waller* (n. 3).

1. The History in the French-speaking Countries in Western and Central Africa

In Western and Central Africa, the process of decolonization from France unfolded in an overall peaceful and consensual manner. The 1958 referendum, introduced by General de Gaulle, established the Fifth Republic in France with the 4th October 1958, constitution. Title XII of the new constitution established the Franco-African Community. This Community replaced the 1946 Union française. It included all former French colonies. They acceded to sovereignty but still had to share their foreign and defence policies with France. One notable exception: Guinea Conakry which became the Republic of Guinea. At the instigation of Ahmed Sékou Touré, deputy and mayor of Conakry, the referendum was massively rejected following a strong disagreement with General de Gaulle. It led to a lasting and damaging quarrel between Guinea and France.

This Franco-African Community never materialized. In fact, it disappeared in 1960, although the twelfth Title of the Constitution was abrogated much later.

At this point, two schools of thoughts, with opposite ideas arose. On the one hand, the Group of Casablanca considered that the newly independent nations had to build their future without dwelling on their despised colonial past, a sort of "cancel culture". On the other hand, the Group of Monrovia considered it was better to capitalize on what had been acquired during the colonization period, especially the regional legal and economic environment that prevailed before the independence[5].

As could be expected, the radical group of Casablanca was predominant. Each country followed its own path. The regional blocs did not stick to their common legal rules inherited from colonization. However, and this is a paradox, most of their leaders were extremely vocal in their commitment to Pan-Africanism. They praised both a proud and conquering national independence, as well as a continental unity with a strong and united African nation. The Organization of African Unity (OAU) was established in 1963 in Addis Ababa[6]. It was – fortunately – founded on the principle of the intangibility of borders. However, in truth, the independence gave little concrete consideration to the Pan-African ideology[7]. This led to the fragmentation of a large part of the continent, including French-speaking Africa, with the emergence of radical and strong nationalist groups.

[5] See https://oau60.au.int/en/pan-africanist-movement-and-road-liberation (last visited on 10th July 2025).

[6] See https://oau60.au.int/en/commemorating-60-years-africas-pan-african-organisation (last visited on 10th July 2025); *Jean A. Penda Matipé*, 'The History of the Hamonisation of Laws in Africa', in: Marta S. Tumnde et al. (eds.), Unified Business Laws for Africa: Common Law Perspectives on OHADA (2009), 7, 18.

[7] *Penda Matipé* (n. 6), 13.

Of course, there were some attempts to merge nations, or to establish new economic solidarities: for instance, the Fédération du Mali was created in 1959 to merge Senegal and Mali; it lasted just a few months. Numerous customs unions or regional structures for cooperation also came into existence. However, these initiatives most often turned out to be disappointing.

Finally, the community of the CFA franc currency, the West African and Central African monetary unions, remained the only tangible shared foundations of economic and monetary cooperation.

This race for sovereignty naturally led to the fragmentation of national laws and, inevitably, given the small sizes of African economies, to their marginalization.

At this point, Kéba Mbaye[8] begins to make history. He was a prominent judge in Senegal educated at the *École normale supérieure William Ponty* of French West Africa, a prestigious college at the time located in Saint-Louis (Senegal). And later, along with Abdou Diouf, who would become in 1981 President of the Republic of Senegal, he was part of the last class of *l' Ecole Nationale de la France d'Outremer.* This school was designed to train territory administrators. It closed its doors in 1959.

Aware of the inevitable decline of national laws, Kéba Mbaye suggested the creation of the African and Mauritian Office for Law Research and Studies (*BAMREL* in French) which led to the signing of a Treaty in 1975. Unfortunately, this *BAMREL* experience was disappointing and quickly abandoned. It was premature. The euphoria sparked by independence was still very strong. Laws stemming from colonization continued to exist within a national framework.

African economies still experienced a strong and continuous growth thanks to high exchange rates for raw materials and to the abundancy of external financing; moneylenders and banks considered that a nation could not go bankrupt.

2. The Ramifications of the Debt Crisis

This euphoria was short-lived: starting in the eighties, the debt crisis began. It spread quickly and fiercely throughout Africa, following the collapse of the exchange rates for raw materials.

Then, a general mistrust in African economies set in. The community of the CFA franc currency, the only tangible link to an economic unity was attacked on all fronts: funds fled the countries, and companies, national or international investors, fled the continent. Economies collapsed. States went bankrupt.

---

[8] *Humphrey Sipalla*, 'Towards an African professional history of international law: The life and work of Kéba Mbaye', in: Frans Viljoen et al. (eds.), Exploring African approaches to international law: Essays in honour of Kéba Mbaye (2022), 13.

One of the reasons for the crisis – of course not the only one, but a significant one – was the loss of confidence of investors. They abandoned the continent, due to the public debt crisis and also due to a business and legal climate which had become a nightmare.

Business law in Africa had indeed become a patchwork of rules over the years. Business legal regulations, which were previously identical, had lost their regional coherence. International donors (World Bank, ...) did not give any consideration to consolidating the rule of law on a regional scale. Because of this piecemeal approach, African business laws had lost their unity. Often inaccessible, they were obsolete and ill-adapted.

In practice, these laws were not adequately taught in African universities. In fact, laws and regulations from former colonizers, which were of course no longer applicable, continued to hold precedence.

This decline of African laws automatically resulted in a decline in case law. Judicial insecurities added up to legal insecurity. Rulings had become unpredictable. They were too often obtained by unscrupulous litigants, taking advantage of the human weaknesses of low-income judges. These abuses became even easier as the application of the legal rule was no longer overseen by a clear and supreme case law. Some judges did not even hesitate to openly refer to the European countries' case laws, even if it had no legal value and dealt with different factual backgrounds.

Therefore, political independence in 1960 did not result in the establishment of sovereign national business laws. Quite the contrary.

Faced with this catastrophic situation threatening their common currency, the Ministers of Finance of the Franc Zone reacted with energy. They decided to strengthen their common currency. They swiftly moved towards ensuring that this currency became supported by common rules in key sectors of economic life: common banking regulations with regional supervisory authorities; a single insurance code relying on a common supervision, the Inter-African Conference on Insurance Markets (CIMA); an Inter-African Conference on Social Security (CIPRES), the creation of the West African Economic and Monetary Union (UEMOA or WAEMU) and of the Economic and Monetary Community of Central Africa (CEMAC).

To complete this process of strengthening their common currency and re-establishing legal security in their regions, the governments decided to lean their monetary community against a unified system of business laws.

III. The OHADA Reform

This was the launching of the OHADA reform: it started with the meeting of finance ministers of the Franc Zone in Ouagadougou on 25th April 1991.

The process quickly took shape. Judge Kéba Mbaye, father of the *BAMREL* reform, was tasked to implement the project. In the wake of independence, Kéba Mbaye had pursued a prestigious career: former first Vice-President of the Hague International Court of Justice, First Vice-President of the International Olympic Committee, founding father of the African Charter on Human and Peoples' Rights – adopted in 1981 at Nairobi – and President of the Senegal Constitutional Council[9]. Commissioned by the Heads of State, his professional journey and his prestigious stature made him the architect of the reform.

He gathered a team of prominent lawyers. He invited the Heads of State to sign the OHADA treaty, to which was attached a first OHADA business law Code. It was a collection of Uniform Acts dealing with companies' activities: Uniform Act on Commercial Companies; Uniform Act on Security Interests and Guarantees; Uniform Act on General Commercial Law; Uniform Act organizing Simplified Recovery Procedures and Enforcement Measures; Uniform Act on Bankruptcy Proceedings; Uniform Act on Accounting Law and Financial Reporting; Uniform Act on Arbitration.

1. The Institutions of the Treaty[10]

The treaty was signed in Port-Louis, Mauritius, on 17th October 1993 on the fifth Summit of French-speaking countries. It established four institutions:

First, a Council of Ministers for Justice and Finance; a legislative authority with strong powers, inspired by the regulation of Article 189 of the Treaty of Rome: Europäische Verordnung (Règlement) and not Richtlinie (Directive).

This institution is key to the success of OHADA: direct applicability of the Acts passed by the Council of Ministers; prevalence of these Acts over preceding and subsequent national rules. The treaty was complemented during the 12th Francophonie Summit in Québec on 17th October 2008, with the creation of a Council of Heads of State.

The second institution is the Common Court of Justice and Arbitration whose headquarters are in Abidjan (Ivory Coast). It is a genuine Supreme Court for Business matters, a final Court of Cassation, establishing the rule of law and judging as a last resort court on the substance of any dispute submitted to it. This court is a pivotal instrument. It gave its full force, its teeth, to the OHADA reform. Its smooth functioning is the biggest challenge for the future of OHADA.

---

[9] *Sipalla* (n. 8); https://www.icj-cij.org/index.php/node/4105 (last visited on 10 July 2025).

[10] Article 27 et seq. OHADA Treaty 2008; see for more information: *Boris Martor et al.*, Business Law in Africa: OHADA and the Harmonization Process, 2nd ed. (2002), 5–15; https://www.ohada.com/l-ohada/institutions-de-l-ohada.html (last visited on 10th July 2025).

The third institution is the Regional School of Magistrates whose headquarters are in Porto Novo (Benin). It is designed to train the magistrates on the new law.

Finally, a permanent Secretariat of the Council of Ministers was established whose headquarters are in Yaoundé (Cameroon). It is designed to handle the administration of the Organization.

2. *The Signatories and the Members-to-be*

All the 15 nations in the Franc Zone were signatories of the treaty. General Lansana Conté, President of Guinea Conakry – a non-member country of the Franc Zone – also signed the treaty. He was encouraged to do so by the Senegalese diplomatic corps, particularly active and involved in the matter.

Quickly ratified by Parliaments, the new OHADA uniform law came into effect, in accordance with the provisions of the Treaty, on 1st January 1998. 1998 was indeed a big bang for the economies, the new single business law wiped out the old rules inherited from colonization. Within a two-year period, all businesses had to adapt their statutes and accounting procedures.

It was a true and unprecedented legal revolution, implemented on a large part of the Continent: a single business and accounting law, modern and adapted to current needs, replaced overnight a patchwork of isolated rules, most of them essentially dating back to the end of the 19th century.

Naturally, this legal revolution provoked a shock and resistance especially on the part of national supreme courts.

However, over a short period, two years, the superiority of this new single business law over the former fragmented national laws was acknowledged. The clear benefits of a common business legal environment, as opposed to isolated national laws, became established. The enthusiasm of the youth, the instant rise of the doctrine, the dozens, then hundreds and thousands of textbooks and publications on the new law eventually overcame fear, reluctance and conservatism. All of this led to the success of OHADA, a success recognized worldwide.

The Democratic Republic of Congo, one of the largest countries in Africa, the size of Europe, covering 3 million sq. km and gathering nearly 100 million inhabitants, officially joined OHADA in September 2012: the OHADA uniform law thus replacing the royal decrees of King Leopold II from the 1870's.

OHADA currently unites 17 nations, over 300 hundred million people, hundreds of thousands of corporations and entrepreneurs[11]. Madagascar and Burundi are about to join the OHADA unified legal framework. Other countries

---

[11] See https://www.ohada.com/l-ohada/etats-membres-de-l-ohada.html (last visited on 10th July 2025); *Mohammed B. Idris*, 'Hamonization of Business Laws in Africa – An Insight into the Laws, Issues, Problems and Prospects', in: Marta S. Tumnde et al. (eds.), Unified Business Laws for Africa: Common Law Perspectives on OHADA (2009), 21, 22.

shall follow suit, probably Portuguese speaking countries at first, following Guinea Bissau's example as a member of the OHADA. Mozambique could take the lead in the process. A group of highly regarded Mozambican legal experts have indeed decided to work towards bringing their huge country closer to OHADA, along with Madagascar and the Union of the Comoros, a founding member of OHADA.

Morocco also shows a strong interest for OHADA, given the growing importance of the country in the continent. However, Moroccan law is rendered in the name of the Prophet and necessarily in the language of the Koran, Arabic. In any case, Morocco supports OHADA and will certainly play a part in the translation of the OHADA norms in legal Arabic.

Kéba Mbaye's ambition, especially embedded in the OHADA treaty, was for OHADA to include as many African countries as possible, if not the whole continent. OHADA is indeed designed to be the engine of continental unity, something always aspired to and desired by Africa. The creation of the African continental free trade area (*Zone de libre-échange continentale africaine*) could, if it were to eventually materialize, encourage this legal and commercial African unity, Kéba Mbaye dreamt of.

Hopefully, OHADA will enable Africa to overcome the *summa divisio* mentioned earlier, by opening up to the English-speaking common law countries[12]. It is worth noting that the English-speaking part of Cameroon is already part of the OHADA[13].

In terms of the substantive law, the OHADA unified legal corpus has been modernized through a review of the Uniform Acts. Also, it has been enriched with new Uniform Acts, such as the Uniform Act relating to Contracts for the Carriage of Goods by Road; the Uniform Act of NGO's and Not-for-Profit Entities accounting; and the Uniform Act pertaining to Mediation.

There is the www.ohada.com website which is the most important OHADA database and worth visiting.

IV. And where do we stand in Europe?

What do these African experiences mean for Europe? Would a European business code make sense, and could Europe follow the example of Africa with OHADA?

---

[12] *Martor et al.* (n. 10), 17.

[13] See for more information on Cameroon: *Martha S. Tumnde*, 'Cameroon offers a Contextual Approach to Unterstanding the OHADA Treaty and Uniform Acts', in: Marta S. Tumnde et al. (eds.), Unified Business Laws for Africa: Common Law Perspectives on OHADA (2009), 45.

It seems clear that it is not so simple; the big bang, tabula rasa approach adopted for OHADA, is clearly not an option, with all our European countries having their commercial laws dating back for centuries.

Nonetheless, with the Treaty of Rome, the Single European Act, and the Treaty of Maastricht, Europe decided to establish economic unity through the creation of a single market, with its four freedoms, and a fifth one, a single currency, intended to complete this economic unity.

As Matthias Lehmann already pointed out, a crucial component is missing in our economic and monetary union. A unified commercial law would give its full force to the single market. It would render our continent more competitive with respect to other huge world markets. It would strengthen our common currency, the Euro.

Today, according to an inventory of European business law conducted in 2016 by the Henri Capitant Association and published in German, English and French, there is, in truth and as no one could suspect, no genuine European business and commercial law, despite the considerable legislative work carried out by the European Commission over the past 65 years[14].

European business law – with the exception of certain areas such as competition law, trademark and patent law, financial and banking law – does not really exist, contrary to other trading blocs: America, China, India... The European legislator has left aside what constitutes the economic engine of Europe: millions of small and middle-sized companies (*mittelständische Unternehmen*).

European business law remains fragmented, difficult to access and outstandingly intricate. Despite the vision of its founding fathers – especially its first president, Walter Hallstein – Europe did not manage to establish company law or commercial law as a foundation for unity, unlike the United States with the Uniform Commercial Code, and Africa with OHADA.

It is time to address this shortcoming in the construction of our Union. In their reports, Enrico Letta and Mario Drahi acknowledge this unfortunate reality[15]. They both recommend the optional 28th regime as a way forward for a number of legal instruments: the Simplified European Company (Die Vereinfachte Europäische Gesellschaft), or the innovative European Company, the Euroguarantee, the European loan contract, the European insurance contract... all of them prerequisites for the implementation of the European capital market union.

---

[14] *Association Henri Capitant*, La construction européenne en droit des affaires, acquis et perspectives, 2016; see also: https://www.henricapitant.org/actions/draft-european-business-code/ (last visited on 10th July 2025).

[15] *Letta* (n. 2); *Mario Draghi*, 'The Draghi report: A competitiveness strategy for Europe (Part A)', September 2024, access the report at: https://commission.europa.eu/topics/eu-competitiveness/draghi-report_en (last visited on 10th July 2025).

V. Conclusion

As a conclusion, business law unification is now an ongoing process in Europe. Its implementation is entrusted to the new Commission, following the recommendations of Enrico Letta and Mario Draghi; it is fully part of the program of Mrs. von der Leyen. Let us hope for the best. The future of our continent is at stake.

General commercial and commercial companies' law in the OHADA and EU

Gérard Ngoumtsa Anou

I. Introduction

This conference paper takes a comparative look at the general commercial and commercial companies' law in the OHADA[1] and the European Union[2].

The true nature of OHADA law[3] has already become clear[4]: Much more than a harmonized law, it is a uniform business law. The field of this business law as provided for by the OHADA treaty is vast[5]. Article 2 of the treaty provides in this sense that:

> "For the purpose of the Treaty, business law shall include all regulations relating to company law, the definition and classification of traders, recovery procedures, measures of enforcement, liquidation and administration proceedings, arbitration, labour law, accounting law, carriage and sales of goods, and any such other matters that the Council of Ministers shall unanimously decide, to include in accordance with the object of the Treaty and the provisions of Article 8 below".

In this enumeration, it appears that the first two subjects cited are corporate law and commercial law. We understand why the Uniform Act on General Commercial Law and the Uniform Act on Commercial Companies (below UA on

---

[1] Some books use "OHBLA", which means Organization for The Harmonization of Business Law in Africa. For general publications in English, see *Boris Martor et al.*, Business Law in Africa OHADA and the Harmonization Process, London, 2nd ed., GMB Publishing Ltd, 2007; *Claire Moore Dickerson* (ed.), Unified Business Laws for Africa, London, GMB Publishing Ltd, 2009.

[2] See *Louis Vogel*, European Business Law, Brussels, Bruylant, Lawlex collection, 2020.

[3] See e.g., *Gérard Ngoumtsa Anou*, Répertoire droit des sociétés, v° OHADA – Droit des sociétés commerciales et du groupement d'intérêt économique, Paris, Dalloz, 2024; *A. Akam Akam et V. Bakreo*, Droit des sociétés commerciales OHADA, Paris, L'Harmattan, 2017; *Benoît Le Bars*, International Arbitration and Corporate Law: An OHADA Practice, The Hague, Eleven International Publishing, 2014; *Akuété Pedro Sando et al.*, OHADA-Droit commercial general, Poitiers, Juriscope, 2020.

[4] On the OHADA nature, see *Gérard Ngoumtsa Anou*, Jurisclasseur droit international, fasc. 170, OHADA-Présentation générale, Paris, LexisNexis, 2018.

[5] On this scope, see *Francis Womdjou*, 'L'échange d'arguments autour de l'élaboration du droit économique à partir du Traité mettant en commun les listes des matières d'affaires', Uniform Law Review 24/3 (2019), 484 et seq.

GCL and UA on CC) were the very first texts adopted by OHADA in 1997. But what is meant by general commercial law and company law?

There is no OHADA text which defines what the term general commercial law means. However, a uniform act relating to general commercial law was adopted in 1997 and was reformed in December 2010[6]. The analysis of questions treated by this text shows that general commercial law according to OHADA legislation is a set of heterogeneous matters including the status of traders, the regime of their activity and some commercial contracts.

Regarding commercial company law, it refers to all the rules applicable to commercial companies. The commercial nature of a company is determined by its form or object, according to Article 6 UA on CCL[7]. There is also a uniform act on cooperative companies[8]. But within the restricted framework of this work, we will only present commercial law and commercial companies' law.

Analysis of these two regulations reveals that they were in several aspects inspired by EU law, both in their content and in the harmonization methods used. But what is the extent of this influence? Is it or could it be reciprocal? Indeed, the technique of the uniform act as it was described by the previous speaker includes characteristics inspired by EU regulations: *the uniform act has direct and immediate effect* on the territory of the Member States; it also enjoys primacy over the domestic law of member states. On the other hand, it does not apply to an economic community. There is therefore no limitation of its scope based on the requirements of an internal market like subsidiarity or proportionality[9].

The uniform acts on commercial law and commercial companies, however, retain certain specificities which could be useful in the reflection with a view to a European business code or a European business law. This can be seen from at least three points of view: firstly, with regard to general commercial law (I) sec-

---

[6] Uniform act on general commercial law, adopted on 1997 and revised on 15th December 2010, OHADA Official Journal, 15th February 2011, 1 et seq.

[7] Uniform Act on Commercial Companies and Economic Interest Groupings, adopted on 17th April 1997 and revised on 30th January 2014, OHADA Official Journal, special Edition, 4th February 2014, 1 et seq. – See the special file 'Droit des sociétés commerciales OHADA rénové: un atout pour les investissements en Afrique', Droit et patrimoine review, 2014, no. 239; see also Penant review 887 (2014), 151 et seq., special edition "Le nouvel acte uniforme sur le droit des sociétés commerciales".

[8] Uniform act on cooperative companies, adopted on 15th December 2010, OHADA Official Journal, 15th February 2011, 1 et seq.; *Tadjudje, Willy*, 'Harmonization (or rather Standardization) of Cooperative Law in the OHADA Zone: What is the Result after Ten Years of Implementation of the Uniform Act?', Revista Jurídica de Economía Social y Cooperativa 39 (2022), 67.

[9] See e. g. *Christian Hillgruber*, 'The Principle of Subsidiarity in European Law', in: Martin Schlag, Boglárka Koller (eds.), Rethinking Subsidiarity, Heidelberg, Springer, 2024, 183 et seq.

ondly with respect to the content of commercial company law (II) and thirdly regarding the scope of application of this law (III).

II. Content of OHADA commercial law and EU law: increased unification of OHADA commercial law

First of all, let us consider the content of OHADA commercial law in order to appreciate its level of unification and possible reciprocal influences.

The harmonization achieved in the OHADA area is more extensive than that of the EU, while EU law serves as a source of inspiration. This concerns several topics. Let us just take two domains to evaluate whether there is reciprocal influence between the two systems: the register of trade and securities, and commercial contracts.

1. Reform of the OHADA register of trade and securities and the European Business Register model

On the first point, i.e. the register, natural or legal persons carrying out an economic activity in an OHADA country in the form of an individual trader, entrepreneur or commercial company must also register in a public register managed by the courts or authorities of each Member State[10]. This is the register of trade and securities provided for by books 2 to 5 UA on GCL. The information recorded with each court or authority is centralized on a national register in each Member State. Then, a regional register centralizes information from national registers in the regional register managed by the Common Court of justice and arbitration of OHADA[11].

This register is intended for public information. It therefore facilitates transparency in economic circles and allows an operator established in a Member State to have information on operators established in other Member States. In each Member State, the register of trade and securities in the local courts and the national register may be managed either in a paper version or in a digital version. This choice depends on the level of digitalization of public services in that State[12]. The formalities carried out with this register by economic operators can be in a paper version or in a digital version. When an operator chooses to make its registrations electronically, the documents are provided partially or com-

[10] See *Paul Lendongo et Kossi Ayate*, Guide pratique de gestion du Registre du Commerce et du Crédit Mobilier (RCCM) et du Registre des Sociétés Coopératives (RSCOOP) dans l'espace OHADA, Porto-Novo, Editions de l'ERSUMA, 2020.

[11] Article 36 UA on GCL.

[12] Article 80 UA on GCL.

pletely electronically[13]. According to Articles 97 et seq., economic operators can also obtain information in electronic form.

This business register preceded the European model, the European Business Register[14], which allows information to be obtained online. Its digitalization was introduced following the reform of the UA on GCL of December 2010. The European register was set up following a directive of June 2012 on the interconnection of central, commercial and company registers[15]. And it was later that the technical specifications and procedures necessary for this interconnection of national trade registers were established.

The interconnection planned by OHADA, then by the EU, allows better access to information on the situation of businesses. It improves the legal certainty of cross-border operations such as restructurings, mergers and acquisitions involving companies from several Member States. But unlike the all-electronic European model, the OHADA regional register can receive information in a paper version. It is not possible to demand that everything be done digitally. This is due to several reasons: the lower literacy rate of the population, the very large number of economic operators in the informal sector and the limited computerization of public services in OHADA countries.

The register of trade and securities in OHADA countries is therefore inspired by French law, but its regional register preceded that of the EU and adapts to local realities.

2. The specific supervision of some main commercial contracts

On the second point, i. e. contracts, the UA on GCL provides for a regime of some business contracts[16]. This is the case for leasing for professional use, the transfer of business assets, commercial sales or even agency. Some of these contracts are inspired by French law, such as the transfer of business assets. Others have a regime more adapted to African realities, such as leasing for professional use.

Agency is the main topic of Book 7 UA on GCL. Its regime was inspired, at least in part, by the UNIDROIT convention on agency. But OHADA commercial agency law is much more inspired by an EU directive, the 1986 directive on

---

13 Article 86 UA on GCL.

14 See https://www.ebr.lv/en/ (last visited on 10th July 2025).

15 Directive 2012/17/EU of the European Parliament and of the Council of 13th June 2012 amending Council Directive 89/666/EEC and Directives 2005/56/EC and 2009/101/EC of the European Parliament and of the Council on the interconnection of central, commercial and company registers.

16 See *Eustache Da Allada*, Le traitement des contrats d'affaires par le droit OHADA, Aix-en-Provence, Presses universitaires d'Aix Marseille, 2022; *Yelian Leonce Frédi Kolimedje*, La théorie générale des contrats d'affaires dans l'espace OHADA, Paris, Thesis University of Paris I, 2018.

agency, which gave rise to some decisions of the EU Court of Justice[17]. OHADA therefore took the EU as an example but went further by providing a uniform text where there is simple harmonization in the EU. It also provided for the international mandatory rules while within the EU it was the Court of Justice which declared the protection of agents internationally mandatory. This was in the so-called Ingmar case in 2000[18]. Let us appreciate an example which shows this influence of EU law: Article 15(5) of the directive is repeated almost word for word by Article 229(2) UA on GCL:

Article 17 § 5 of the EU directive of 1986: "5. The commercial agent shall lose his entitlement to the indemnity in the instances provided for in paragraph 2 or to compensation for damage in the instances provided for in paragraph 3, if within one year following termination of the contract he has not notified the principal that he intends pursuing his entitlement".

Article 229 § 2 UA on GCL: "The commercial agent shall lose the right to compensation where he failed to notify the principal that he intends to enforce his right through a notice served by the bailiff or by any means showing actual receipt by the principal, within a period of one year after termination of the contract".

A second example is provided by Article 18 of the EU directive which was reproduced almost word for word in Article 230 UA on GCL.

Article 18 of EU directive:
"The indemnity or compensation referred to in Article 17 shall not be payable:
(b) where the commercial agent has terminated the agency contract, *unless such termination is justified by circumstances attributable to the principal or on grounds of age, infirmity or illness of the commercial agent* in consequence of which he cannot reasonably be required to continue his activities".
Article 230 AU on GCL:
"The compensatory allowance provided for in the foregoing shall not be due:
2) in case of termination of the contract at the agent's initiative, *unless such termination is justified by circumstances attributable to the principal or not caused by age, infirmity or illness of the commercial agent*, and more generally, by circumstances independent of the will of the agent as a result of which the continuation of his activity cannot be reasonably required".

As we can see, OHADA commercial law has a diversity of sources of inspiration. It is partly inspired by French law. The uniform act concerns "general commercial law", a rather evocative term since Book 1 of the French commercial code is entitled "On commerce in general". It is also inspired by EU law, particularly with regard to agency law. At the same time, the OHADA regional

[17] Council Directive 86/653/EEC of 18th December 1986 on the coordination of the laws of the Member States relating to self-employed commercial agents.
[18] ECJ of 9th November 2000, case C-381/98, Ingmar GB Ltd v Eaton Leonard Technologies Inc.

commercial register preceded that of the EU and it is controlled by a single institution, the Common Court of Justice and Arbitration.

Finally, some parts of this OHADA commercial law are inspired by international conventions such as the Vienna CISG or the UNIDROIT convention on agency.

III. More substantial unification of OHADA commercial company law

In the field of corporate law, an observation similar to that which was made regarding commercial law can be reported. OHADA law is partly inspired by EU law, but it is more unified and more comprehensive than European company law. We can appreciate it regarding two points, the rules applicable to companies, and the forms of commercial companies.

1. The almost total unification of the OHADA rules applicable to companies

Concerning the first point, i. e. the rules, Companies have been the subject of two uniform acts within OHADA: the Uniform Act relating to the law of cooperative companies and the Uniform Act on commercial companies and economic interest groupings, revised in January 2014. The original 1997 text was already a remarkable progress compared to the previous state of law in member countries. It was inspired by French law no. 66-537 of 24th July 1966 on commercial companies.

The AUSCGIE has unified and improved the content of commercial company law, both with regard to general rules and with regard to special rules. This text includes general uniform rules on the creation of commercial companies (book 1), on their operations (book 2), on the civil liability of the company management (book 3), on legal relations between companies (book 4), on the transformation of companies (book 5), on mergers and partial contribution of assets (book 6), on the dissolution and liquidation of companies (book 7), on the invalidity of the company and company acts (book 8), on formalities and publicities (book 9) and finally on open-end capital (book 10).

As such, this law is essentially inspired by French law which is itself partially inspired by EU law through the transposition of directives. Certain solutions provided for by EU law are found directly or indirectly in OHADA law.

It is much more uniform and much more comprehensive than that of the EU which only covers sectoral aspects of company law.

With regard to EU law, various rules have been adopted in the form of directives, more rarely in the form of regulations. They are based on Articles 50 and

54 of the TFEU. Their objective is to remove obstacles to the freedom of establishment.

Among the general rules of the EU, we can mention those relating to the harmonization of the conditions for creating public limited companies in the Member States, or the harmonization of the rules applicable to invalidity. Other directives concern the functioning of companies, more particularly transparency in companies or corporate governance[19].

Finally, other directives concern company restructuring, in particular mergers and acquisitions.

But some EU texts have greater ambition with regard to the number of corporate law issues they address: this is the case with the Directive of June 2017 relating to certain aspects of company law[20]. It covers issues as varied as the creation of companies and their invalidity, publicity and the interconnection of central trade and company registers, the maintenance and modification of share capital and even mergers.

An example is Article 46 of this directive which provides that an undertaking to perform work or supply services may not form part of the assets. Article 389(5) UA on CCL provides the same thing. Likewise, Article 49 of the directive on the need to produce a report from experts on contributions other than in cash is a rule that already existed in OHADA law[21].

In terms of accounting, the EU has tried to harmonize the rules on company accounting[22] while OHADA has a body of uniform rules applicable to business accounting. From one member country to another, the same accounting standards apply. This unification was realized by a uniform act on accounting law.

Finally, without claiming to be exhaustive, we could cite the use of digital processes in company law, the subject of directives of the EU[23]. Most of these issues on which the EU is content with harmonized and fragmented rules have been the subject of OHADA rules that are both uniform and more complete. In the OHADA uniform act, references to the use of digital processes are diffuse in the text.

---

[19] See *Association Henri Capitant*, The Integration of European Business Law: acquis and outlook, Paris, LGDJ, 2016.

[20] Directive (EU) 2017/1132 of the European Parliament and of the Council of 14th June 2017 relating to certain aspects of company law (Text with EEA relevance).

[21] Article 400 UA on CCL (AUSCGIE).

[22] See Article 49 UA on CCL.

[23] See Directive (EU) 2025/25 of the European Parliament and of the Council of 19 December 2024 amending Directives 2009/102/EC and (EU) 2017/1132 as regards further expanding and upgrading the use of digital tools and processes in company law (Text with EEA relevance); Directive (EU) 2019/1151 of the European Parliament and of the Council of 20th June 2019 amending Directive (EU) 2017/1132 as regards the use of digital tools and processes in company law (Text with EEA relevance).

2. *Diversification and modernization of company forms*

Regarding the second point, i.e. company forms, rules applicable to every specific type of company, OHADA law provides for a uniform regime for the main types of companies admitted in this area. It also provides the freedom to transfer a head office to another member country. Among the types of companies covered almost entirely are the general partnership, the limited partnership, the limited liability company, the public limited company, the simplified joint stock company, the joint stock company and the de facto company.

On the contrary, in EU countries, only a few specific companies have been the subject of a harmonization effort. The Union was able, through regulations, to create the European company (SE) or even the European Cooperative Society (SCE) and the European Economic Interest Grouping (EEIG). But the number of European companies created since then does not suggest that this is a success worth replicating. At most, we can consider that it may have encouraged the institution of single-member limited liability companies in member countries. This can also explain the hope or discussions on the opportunity and relevance of a European business code[24].

Observation of the application of this law shows greater integration of the OHADA space.

IV. The application of OHADA commercial and companies' law and EU law: An essential difference regarding the scope of application

From the point of view of the implementation of commercial law and company law, the comparison between the EU and OHADA is more contrasted. EU law has a broader scope of application. But it is less deep than that of the OHADA system both regarding material and spatial scope of application.

1. *Material scope of application*

As regarding firstly the material scope of application, OHADA commercial law and corporate law have a scope of application different from that of the EU. This is due to several causes.

[24] See on this idea *Laurence Idot*, 'À propos de l'avant-projet de Code européen des affaires', Europe no. 2, Février 2024, information (alerte) 11; *Philippe Dupichot*, 'Le projet de code européen des affaires', Recueil Dalloz 2022, 744 et seq.; *Remy Cabrillac*, 'Un Code européen des affaires, une chance pour la construction européenne', Recueil Dalloz 2019, 1191 et seq.; *Benoît Lecourt*, 'Rapport sur l'élaboration d'un code européen des affaires', Revue des sociétés 2019, 711 et seq.; *Louis Vogel*, 'Pour un Code européen des affaires', Recueil Dalloz 2018, 1688 et seq.; with critical analysis *Louis D'Avout*, 'L'étonnante initiative en faveur d'un code européen des affaires', La Semaine Juridique – Edition Générale 21/22 (2019), act. 559.

The first cause is the difference in nature between the two types of organizations. OHADA is a legal integration organization and it is not an economic community with a market. The EU is an economic community with a single market. Its business law is designed to meet the management needs of this market. Thus, competition law is one of the very first aspects of European commercial law that was addressed. Still on the subject of the market, there are significant achievements by the EU in consumer law. On the other hand, in Africa there is a simple preliminary draft of an OHADA uniform act on the consumer contract which has never been adopted.

This EU law covers more disparate areas of commercial law and company law: market law, in particular competition and consumer law, electronic commerce law, intellectual property law, financial markets, prudential rules applicable to banking companies and insurance, creation of capital companies, restructuring of companies, corporate governance, etc.

OHADA, for its part, is established in a space where there are already several pre-existing economic communities. These communities address issues related to their respective regional common markets: competition, banks, investments, etc. These are CEMAC (*Economic and Monetary Community of Central Africa*), UEMOA (*West African Economic and Monetary Union*), CEDEAO (*Economic community of West African states*, ECOWAS) and CEEAC (*Economic Community of Central African States, ECCAS*) among others[25]. Furthermore, other business law matters fall under the jurisdiction of legal integration organizations competing with OHADA in the same regional area. This is the case with regard to intellectual property which is part of commercial law within the meaning of French law, but falls under the jurisdiction of the African Intellectual Property Organization (OAPI) and not OHADA. This is also the case for insurance, which falls under the Inter-African Conference of Insurance Markets (CIMA). OHADA, although it has the possibility of expanding the field of commercial law and corporate law, is content with a few large areas. However, it harmonizes them more thoroughly than the EU does: status of the trader and entrepreneur; commercial registers, commercial contracts, commercial companies, etc.

The second cause is the legal basis for the harmonization of law. Article 2 of the OHADA Treaty leaves a wide margin of appreciation to the Council of Ministers while EU countries are bound by a strict sharing of competences between the EU and the Member States. This distribution is also based on the principles of subsidiarity and proportionality which do not exist within OHADA. These principles limit the possibility for the EU to unify its commer-

[25] See *C. Mba Owono*, Droit communautaire des affaires de la CEMAC, Paris, LGDJ, 2016; *Moussa Dougoune*, Droit des affaires OHADA – UEMOA – CEMAC 2017, Paris, Sedec, 2017.

cial and company law in a comprehensive manner. Therefore, it will not be possible to go as far as OHADA without a revision of the European treaties.

A third cause of different material scopes of application is the use of different methods of legal integration. The EU relies heavily on directives. This in principle, results in less integrated texts, but in more areas. OHADA, while adopting the Uniform Acts which have an application mechanism close to that of the EU regulations, has limits. As a limit, there are explicit or implicit references to national laws as well as the provisions of criminal incrimination in the uniform act relating to commercial law or commercial companies. OHADA leaves less room for maneuver to States. This lack of diversity of integration instruments, namely standardization, harmonization and simple coordination, has disadvantages for OHADA. This prevents certain texts from being adopted in the form of directives or model laws that States are reluctant to adopt in the form of uniform rules. There are some illustrations of this: Preliminary draft of the Uniform Act on the consumer contract; preliminary draft of the Uniform Act on the contract.

2. *Scope of application in space*

Secondly, another difference between OHADA commercial and corporate law and that of the EU is their respective scopes of application in space. In principle, EU law is intended to apply to relationships having an impact on the internal market. These often concern cross-border legal relations between Member States or with regard to the EU, which seems normally to exclude purely internal legal relations.

This requirement, linked to the internal market, does not exist in OHADA countries. OHADA is free to regulate internal, intra-community and sometimes international commercial relations as long as this is necessary to improve the business environment[26]. For example, a commercial sale of goods between two traders established in Cameroon is governed by OHADA commercial sales law. A commercial sale between a trader established in Cameroon and a trader established in Guinea is governed by the same OHADA law, because the sale is intra-community. A commercial sale between a Cameroonian company and a German company is also governed by OHADA law on commercial sales according to Article 234(2) of the AUDCG, while both countries are signatories to the CISG and this sale is international within the meaning of the CISG[27].

---

[26] See *Gérard Ngoumtsa Anou*, Droit OHADA et conflits de lois, Paris, LGDJ, 2013, no. 279 et seq.; *Pierre Meyer*, 'Le droit OHADA et le droit international privé: les règles d'applicabilité du droit uniforme', Uniform Law Review 23/1 (2018), 99 et seq.

[27] See *Paul-Gérard Pougoué/Gérard Ngoumtsa Anou*, 'L'applicabilité du nouveau droit OHADA de la vente commerciale et le droit international privé: une réforme inachevée', in:

This being said, the OHADA standards applicable to international legal operations are few in number while the desire to encourage investments and transactions with foreign countries should have led to the adoption of real instruments of private international law such as they exist in the EU with its regulations Brussels I bis, Rome I and Rome II. On this point, it is OHADA which would benefit from learning lessons from the European experience. Commercial law is not only internal. It is also international.

V. Conclusion: What lessons can be learned by the EU from the African experience?

OHADA standards in general commercial law and corporate law are more integrated than those of the EU. They are uniform where those of the EU are mainly harmonized, and therefore less integrated. OHADA rules are also more comprehensive and sometimes cover an entire subject, whereas the EU is content with sectoral rules. This being said, certain OHADA rules are directly inspired by EU law such as the commercial agency regime while others are indirectly inspired by it by using European solutions transposed into French texts. More rarely, we notice that sometimes OHADA plans certain solutions before they are officially enshrined in Europe, such as the interconnection of national commercial registers.

It seems that in areas such as commercial agency, agency or even common company law, it is possible to achieve general harmonization within the EU. The ideal would be a European business law code that facilitates visibility, accessibility and intelligibility. But the idea of a European business code, despite the advantages it can provide in terms of legal certainty, remains at the stage of an idea or project in Europe. It is possible to conclude by the following observations:

- The development of a European business "code" in one go is utopian. It is possible to determine a set of subjects that could be the subject of the European Business Code, but it seems preferable to harmonize them subject by subject with patience. This can be backed by a harmonization program in several stages over periods of several years as within OHADA.
- In the meantime, it is possible to bring together existing texts in a "code" to facilitate readability and intelligibility. To find out the state of EU commercial law on an issue, it is sometimes necessary to consult several texts and even their transposition. This does not facilitate the accessibility of the legal stand-

Dolores Bentolila, Marcelo G. Kohen (eds.), Mélanges offerts à jean Michel Jacquet, Paris, LexisNexis, 2013, 513 et seq.

ard which is a key element of legal certainty. The fact that OHADA texts are uniform and accessible has seriously improved legal certainty.

- Unless there is a revision of the European treaties, it will be difficult, if not impossible, to go as far as OHADA.
- It is possible to go further in the harmonization of general commercial law and company law in Europe (for example, unify the law of commercial contracts based on a comparative study of the existing one; further harmonize the companies regime, even if only between a group of countries at first).
- It is necessary to include specialists of international business law in the reflection on European business law, because they seem to have been excluded so far.

The impact of OHADA's Uniform Act relating to General Commercial Law in non-francophone Africa: The case of the Revised Commercial Code of Ethiopia

Seyoum Yohannes Tesfay

I. Introduction

We attempt, in this contribution, to shed light on the actual and possible impact of OHADA Uniform Acts in non-Francophone Africa. To this end, we briefly introduce Pan-African legal development aimed at economic integration of the continent and the role private law can play in realizing this goal. We then discuss the need for harmonization of commercial law and the role OHADA Uniform Acts play and are likely to play in this regard in non-Francophone Africa. We take, in particular, Ethiopia as a case study focusing on the role of OHADA Uniform Act Relating to General Commercial Law in the revision of the Commercial Code of Ethiopia.

II. Efforts at Pan-African Economic Integration: A Background

Trade in goods and services among African countries has been pitifully low and continues to be so. Available data shows that intra-African trade was about USD 6.9 billion in 1990 while African trade with the rest of the world was about USD 91.6 billion during the same year[1]. There has been a gradual increase since then in the total exports of African countries and the share of intra-African trade though much less than desired[2]. The United Nations Commission for Trade and Development (UNCTAD) report of 2019 shows that intra-African exports accounted for 16.6 % of the total exports of African countries in the year 2017. In contrast, trade among European countries is said to have constituted 68.1 %, among Asian countries 59.4 % and in America 55 % of their total exports during the same year[3].

---

[1] *Shehu Usman Rano Aliyu*, Intra-African Trade Macroeconomic Performance of Africa: Implications for the African Continental Free Trade Area, 8, available at https://mpra.ub.uni-muenchen.de/121436/1/MPRA/_paper_121436.pdf, last visited on 10th July 2025.

[2] *Aliyu* (n. 1).

[3] United Nations Commission for Trade and Development, press release available at https://unctad.org/press-material/facts-figures-0, last visited on 10th July 2025.

African states are acutely aware of the challenges in this regard and have been taking measures to improve trade and investment ties with each other. To this end, a treaty establishing the African Continental Free Trade Area (AfCFTA) was signed in 2018 and entered into force in May 2019. Forty-eight out of the fifty-four signatories had deposited their instrument of ratification as at the 13th August 2024[4]. The treaty aims at the creation of conducive conditions for the integration of the African markets by removing barriers to the free movement of persons, goods, services and capital[5]. The Protocol on Trade in Goods which forms part of the agreement, for instance, aims at the progressive elimination of tariff and non-tariff barriers to trade, the facilitation of customs procedures and attaining enhanced cooperation as regards the reduction of technical barriers to trade such as sanitary and phytosanitary measures[6]. The Protocol on Trade in Services, which similarly forms part of the AfCFTA Agreement aims at the progressive liberalization of trade in services and fostering domestic and foreign investment[7].

III. The Role of Private Law in Development and the Need for Harmonization

In what follows, we will attempt to throw some light on the role private law can play to complement rules of public law nature that aim at economic integration and development of Africa. We will then briefly discuss the need for harmonization of commercial laws to facilitate progress.

1. The Role of Private Law in Development

Though the ratification of the treaty establishing the African Continental Free Trade Area is a welcome development, rules of public international law nature focusing on tariffs and non-tariff measures imposed by states alone are not enough to spur economic growth and integration. They need to be complemented by private law rules that provide a sound legal infrastructure for trade and investment. One of the roles that private law plays in this regard is the balancing of conflicting interests of private parties that engage in a transaction. This could be balancing the interests of a seller and purchaser, landlord and business, em-

---

[4] See https://www.tralac.org/resources/infografic/13795-status-of-afcfta-ratification.html, last visited on 10th July 2025.

[5] Agreement Establishing the African Continental Free Trade Area, signed in Kigali on 21st March 2018, Articles 2, 3 and 4.

[6] Agreement Establishing African Continental Free Trade Area (n. 5), Protocol on Trade in Goods Article 2(2).

[7] Agreement Establishing African Continental Free Trade Area (n. 5), Protocol on Trade in Services, Article 3(2).

ployer and employee, for example[8]. We can think of many other private relationships such as the debtor-creditor, shareholder-company, management-company and creditor and guarantor/mortgagor/pledgor relationships that may be balanced by private law. Besides, private law helps constitute institutions that can be used by business entities or people to shape their legal relationships[9]. Rules regarding legal personality such as conferred on corporations are cases in point. Such rules create a "specific connection between several people that is legally binding and offer legal certainty in their dealings with each other and with third parties"[10].

Having private law rules that optimally balance business relationships and provide enabling infrastructure for investment and trade facilitate development in a more general sense too. Amartya Sen maintains, in this connection, that there is casual interdependence between legal and economic development. He shows this by taking the rise of capitalism as an example. He argues[11]:

[c]apitalism did not emerge until the evolution of law and order and the legal and practical acceptance of property rights had made an ownership-based economy feasible and operational. The efficiency of exchange could not work until contracts could be freely made and effectively enforced, through legal and behavioural reforms. Economic expansions are hard to plan without the needed trust in each other's plans and announcements and the required confidence that agreed arrangements can be relied on.

At a more abstract level, legal and institutional reform should be sought even if this were not to be translated into economic development. Amartya Sen contends[12]:

... [l]egal development is constitutively involved in the development process, and conceptual integrity requires that we see legal development as crucial for the development process itself. That is, even if legal development were not to contribute one iota to economic development [I am not saying this is the case, but even if this were, counterfactually true], even then judicial and legal reform would be a critical part of the development process. The notion of development cannot be conceptually delinked from legal and judicial arrangements.

The essence of his contention above is that through long usage certain content has been attributed to the very idea of development itself. In consequence, "[...] it is impossible to define development independently of those established asso-

---

[8] *Alexander Hallgardt*, The Role of Private Law in Times of Polycrisis, 2024, available at: https://verfassungsblog.de/the-role-of-private-law-in-times-of-polycrisis/, last visited on 10th July 2025.

[9] *Hallgardt* (n. 8).

[10] *Hallgardt* (n. 8).

[11] *Amartya Sen*, What is the Role of Legal and Judicial Reform in the Development Process? The World Bank Legal Review: Law, Equity and Development, 42, available at: https://brill.com/display/book/edcoll/9789047411727/B9789047411727_s004.xml, last visited on 10th July 2025.

[12] *Sen* (n. 11), 38.

ciations"[13]. And one such constitutive part of development is "a basic level of legality and judicial attainment"[14]. The implication of this is that legal reform could be seen in and of itself as progress so long as it leads to a heightened level of legality and judicial attainment even where it does not come with economic dividend.

The foregoing holds true as regards legal reform at the level of each African country. Having modern private-law regimes that facilitate entrepreneurship go a long way in realizing development.

2. *The Need for Harmonization and the Various Approaches to It*

Having modern private business laws at the level of each African country is not, in and of itself, sufficient to attain the desired level of economic development. Even with good domestic laws, the requirements and quirks of a foreign legal system may pose unpleasant surprises to a party engaged in a transnational transaction[15]. Identifying and understanding the laws of a foreign jurisdiction that may apply to the cross-border transaction in whole or in part involve financial costs and delays[16]. In short, legal heterogeneity may act as an obstacle to commerce compelling businesses to incur significant expenses and delays. At worst, it may totally deter parties from engaging in cross-border transactions for fear of such risks[17]. Hence, some contend that the commercial laws of countries within an economic block should afford certainty and predictability to counter parties in different jurisdictions. They go even further and hold that unity of commercial laws is a precondition for a full realization of the benefits of economic blocks. For nations that embark on the creation of "an economic community, the unification of the legal regime concerning business transactions is bound, sooner or later, to become an issue of considerable political importance"[18].

The same holds true for economic integration and development that African countries are trying to attain by forming the Continental African Free Trade Area. Intra-African trade will not grow to the desired level unless the efficiency of exchanges is attained by putting in place private business laws that are at least easy to identify and understand by business counter parts in other jurisdictions.

---

[13] *Sen* (n. 11), 38.

[14] *Sen* (n. 11), 38.

[15] *Asif Efrat*, Promoting Trade through Private Law: Explaining International Legal Harmonization, Review of International Organizations (2016), Vol. 11(3), 4, available at https://papers.ssrn.com/sol3/papers.cfm?abstract_id=3381102, last visited on 10th July 2025.

[16] *Efrat* (n. 15), 4.

[17] *Efrat* (n. 15), 4.

[18] *Reinhard Zimmermann*, Comparative Law and the Europeanization of Private Law, in: Mathias Reimann, Reinhard Zimmermann (eds.), The Oxford Handbook of Comparative Law (2006), 3.

Similarly, free movement of capital in Africa will be difficult in the absence of conducive rules for the organization of enterprises, raising capital and transactions in securities. An effective legal and institutional mechanism for the settlement of commercial disputes within Africa will also be necessary. Cross-border business contracts will not be effectively enforced if African counterparts to such contracts have no option but to arbitrate disputes between them in Paris under the auspices of the ICC or in London under the auspices of the LCIA. In short, some level of the harmonization of commercial laws and a credible dispute settlement mechanism are necessary for the success of the African Continental Free Trade Area.

Harmonization in the context of transnational commercial law refers to the "process of identifying and reconciling differences in legal systems and cultures to create instruments that standardize terms and practices of cross-border trade"[19]. Of course, there are also cases of what one may call "preventive" harmonization. This involves establishing new principles and practices that aim at minimizing divergence when national laws governing new issues are developed. This has been typical in areas of commerce affected by new technologies or novel business practices. The United Nations Commission on International Trade Law (UNCITRAL) Model Law on Electronic Commerce of 1996 may be cited as an example[20].

The types of instruments that result from harmonization exercises vary significantly forming a spectrum. On the softer end of the spectrum, we have standard trade terms for use in a certain industry that contracting parties may choose to incorporate into their contracts[21]. Somewhat in the middle are model "laws" which are templates for legislation that take full account of state sovereignty. They become binding only if a state decides to adopt them as laws. Business laws produced by the United Nations Commission on International Trade Law (UNCITRAL) are, for instance, of this type[22].

Resolutions and directives issued by the European Union (EU) and the OHADA Uniform Act may be said to stand on the harder end of the spectrum. A directive outlines a binding goal that EU member states must attain. Member States are expected to issue their own national laws to reach the goals as outlined in the directive. A European Union resolution, in contrast, is a legislative act, having a binding effect within the domestic legal framework of members of

---

[19] *Loren Turner*, Researching the Harmonization of International Commercial Law (2022), available at: https://www.nyulawglobal.org/globalex/unification_harmonization1.html, last visited on 10th July 2025.

[20] *Jose Faria*, *Estrella Angelo*, Legal Harmonization through Model Laws: The Experience of the United Nations Commission on International Trade Law (UNCITRAL), 11, available at: https://www.justice.gov.za/alraesa/conferences/2005sa/papers/s5_faria2.pdf, last visited on 10th July 2025.

[21] *Turner* (n. 19).

[22] *Faria* (n. 20), 8.

the EU[23]. OHADA Uniform Acts are standardized legislations on business law that are directly applicable in member states. They override any existing domestic legislation that is incompatible with them. They are also more comprehensive in their coverage of business law than EU resolutions and on the stronger end of the spectrum of harmonization instruments[24].

We will, in what follows, briefly dwell on the Uniform Acts to provide a background for the discussion on their impact in non-Francophone Africa.

IV. A Bird's-Eye View of the OHADA Uniform Acts

Established in 1993, the Organization for the Harmonization of Business Law in Africa, OHADA strives to enact harmonized, simple and modern rules that are adopted to the economies of the member countries[25]. The treaty affirms that it aspires to the formation of an African Economic Community – a milestone on the path to African Unity[26]. To this end, OHADA has since its establishment issued eleven uniform acts covering various areas of business law, including the Uniform Act Relating to General Commercial Law, on which we will dwell in detail under section VI below[27]. Another uniform act deals with the organization of business enterprises, commercial companies and economic interest groupings in the parlance of the act[28]. Yet another act comprises rules governing the accounts that must be kept by enterprises run by natural or corporate persons[29]. Three other acts are designed to facilitate debt recovery. One of these is an act that governs the allocation of an asset or property in favour of a creditor to guarantee the discharge of an obligation and the provision of personal security[30]. Another act provides rules for collective proceedings by creditors for the recovery of debts from a debtor prior to or after the occurrence of insolvency[31].

---

[23] *Turner* (n. 19).

[24] *B. Martor*, *N. Pilkington*, Et al, Business Law in Africa: OHADA and the Harmonization Process, 2nd ed., GMB Publishing (2007), 18–22.

[25] Treaty of 17th October 1993 on the Harmonization of Business Law in Africa, Article 1.

[26] See the preamble of the Treaty of 17th October 1993 on the Harmonization of Business Law in Africa.

[27] The other uniform acts include the Uniform Act Relating to Commercial Companies and Economic Interest Groupings, the Uniform Act Organizing Securities, the Uniform Act Organizing Collective Proceedings for Clearing of Debt, the Uniform Act Organizing Simplified Recovery Procedures and Enforcement Measures, the Uniform Act on Harmonization of the Accounts of Enterprises, and the Uniform Act on the Contract for the Carriage of Goods by Road.

[28] Uniform Act Relating to Commercial Companies and Economic Interest Groupings (Lomé 15th December 2010).

[29] Uniform Act on the Harmonization of the Accounts of Enterprises (24th March 2000).

[30] Uniform Act Organizing Securities (Lomé 15th December 2010), Articles 1 and 4.

[31] Uniform Act Organizing Collective Proceedings for Clearing of Debts (1st January 1999).

Yet another of the acts that pertain to debt recovery covers rules that deal with simplified recovery procedures and measures of enforcement such as sequestration and attachment of property and the sale of such property to pay creditors[32].

OHADA has also established a dispute settlement mechanism at the core of which is the Common Court of Justice and Arbitration (CCJA). The court plays the dual role of promoting arbitration and acting as the regional court of last resort ensuring uniform application of the OHADA acts[33]. Besides, two of the nine acts focus on the settlement of commercial disputes through arbitration. The Arbitration Rules of the Common Court of Justice and Arbitration deal with the role of the Common Court of Justice and Arbitration in dispute settlement, the procedure applicable before the said court and the recognition and enforcement of arbitral awards[34]. The Uniform Act on Arbitration governs any arbitration where the seat of the arbitration tribunal is in one of the States Parties to OHADA[35]. It deals with matters such as the composition of arbitral tribunals, arbitral awards, appeals against awards and recognition and enforcement of awards[36]. The ninth OHADA act governs contracts for the carriage of goods by road and applies to cases where either the place of departure or delivery of the goods, as specified in the contract is an OHADA member country[37]. OHADA is really a unique experiment in that it has resulted in the legal integration of the states in the block as far as business laws are concerned[38]. It is also unparalleled in that it has created a judicial system devoted to business law that operates parallel to its analogues in the member states[39]. All the OHADA acts, substantive and dispute settlement related alike, are for historical reasons clearly based on French business law[40].

---

[32] Uniform Act Organizing Simplified Recovery Procedures and Enforcement Measures (Libreville 10th April 1998).

[33] *Claire Moore Dickerson,* Harmonizing Business Laws in Africa: OHADA Calls the Tune, 44 Columbia Journal of Transnational Law (2005), 21.

[34] OHADA Arbitration Rules of the Common Court of Justice (11th March 1999), Articles 1, 2–28 and 29–34 respectively.

[35] OHADA Uniform Act on Arbitration (Ouagadougou, 11th March 1999), Article 1.

[36] Uniform Act on Arbitration (n. 35), Articles 5–8, 19–24, 25–29 and 30–34 respectively.

[37] Uniform Act on the Contract for the Carriage of Goods by Road (Yaoundé, 22nd March 2003), Article 1.

[38] *Renaud Beauchard, Mahutodji Kodo,* Can OHADA Increase Legal Certainty in Africa?, in: World Bank Justice and Development Working Paper Series (2011), 7.

[39] *Dickerson* (n. 33), 64.

[40] *Dickerson* (n. 33), 31.

V. OHADA Well-Positioned to Impact Integration of Commercial Law under the Auspices of the African Continental Free Trade Area

Although OHADA acts were conceived for French speaking African countries, interest in them has grown in non-Francophone Africa. Guinea-Bissau and Equatorial Guinea, countries that speak Portuguese and Spanish respectively, have joined the fold of OHADA.[41] People who were involved in the launching of OHADA have also formed an association named Association for the Unification of Law in Africa (UNIDA) with the aim of spreading knowledge about OHADA acts to non-Francophone Africa. The idea is to harmonize African laws along the lines of OHADA[42].

The establishment of the African Continental Free Trade Area in 2019 is likely to spur interest in OHADA Acts as Africa-wide harmonization of commercial laws gains traction[43]. Obviously, it is too early to tell the level of harmonization and the instruments of harmonization that will be preferred under the framework of the African Continental Free Trade Area. Whatever the level and method of harmonization that may be pursued, OHADA Acts are well positioned to impact the development of commercial laws outside of the OHADA zone for a variety of reasons. That the OHADA Acts have the full force of law in seventeen of the fifty-four African countries gives them the first-mover advantage. Besides, the fact that more than a dozen African countries outside the OHADA zone follow the Civil Law tradition increases the likelihood of their impact. These countries include some of the biggest by population and economic size like Angola, Algeria, Egypt, Ethiopia and Mozambique[44]. Yet other countries like South Africa, Namibia, Botswana, Mauritius and Seychelles follow a mixed system of Civil Law Common Law Systems making them amenable to the influence of OHADA Acts[45]. Some other countries like Morocco and Libya follow a mix of Civil and Islamic Law making them open to the influence of the OHADA Acts[46].

We note at this juncture, that only a dozen African countries are said to follow Common Law Systems. Five of these are effectively surrounded by

---

[41] *Johnathan Bashi Rudahindwa*, OHADA and the Making of Transnational Commercial Law in Africa (2018), Paper presented at Law and Development Conference in Cape Town, 6, available at: https://doi.org/10.1515/ldr-2018-0024, last visited on 10th July 2025.

[42] *Martor* (n. 24), Vi and Vii.

[43] Forty-eight countries have ratified the treaty and seven of them have commenced trading under the agreement as of October 2024. See https://www.reuters.com/legal/legalindustry/investment-africa-free-trade-area-agreement-powers-continents-energy-future-2025-01-17/, last visited on 10th July 2025.

[44] Some sources classify Egypt and Algeria as mixed Civil-Islamic law countries. See https://www.cia.gov/the-world-factbook/field/legal-system/ last visited on 10th July 2025.

[45] See https://juriglobe.ca/eng/sys-juri/class-poli/droi-civil.php, last visited on 10th July 2025.

[46] Id. (n. 45).

OHADA members making trade and economic integration with the latter the more natural phenomenon. For instance, Nigeria is effectively surrounded by Benin, Chad, Niger and Cameroun, all OHADA members while Ghana is surrounded by Togo, Ivory coast and Burkina Faso[47]. The bottom line is that all these factors are likely to increase the impact of OHADA Acts throughout Africa, be that in harmonization of laws under the auspices of the African Continental Free Trade Area or legal reforms undertaken at the initiative of-individual African states.

In what follows, we look at the role they played in the revision of the Commercial Code of Ethiopia, focusing only on the OHADA Act Relating to General Commercial Law by way of example.

VI. OHADA's Uniform Act Relating to General Commercial Law: Its Impact in the Revision of the Ethiopian Commercial Code

In what follows we discuss the choice of the OHADA Act Relating to General Commercial Law as one of the benchmarks for the revision of the Commercial Code of Ethiopia. To this end, we will first dwell on the shared roots of the two laws and then demonstrate conceptual and structural similarities of the OHADA Act and Book I of the 1960 Commercial Code. We then briefly discuss the rationales for this choice.

1. Shared Historical Roots and Genetic Origins

Despite its very long history as a state, Ethiopia had no "legal system" in the sense of a corpus of laws with a formal source that was applied methodically, consistently and throughout its jurisdiction until the mid-twentieth century. The people looked for justice more to the rulers rather than legal institutions and "rules of law"[48]. The *Fetha Negast* (Law of the Kings), which was introduced sometime between the fourteenth and sixteenth century, was not formally promulgated until 1908. In terms of content, its focus was on ecclesiastic issues, marriage, successions and penal rules though it did cover some matters of relevance to commerce such as commercial ventures, sale, purchase, loans, pledge and guarantees[49].

---

[47] *Akin Akinbote*, OHADA Treaty and Law by Anglophone States, 1, available at: https://nigerianlawguru.com/wp-content/uploads/2024/11/OHADA-TREATY-AND-LAW-BY-ANGLOPHONE-STATES.pdf, last visited on 10th July 2025.

[48] *Kenneth Redden*, The Legal system of Ethiopia, The Michie Company Law Publishers, Charlottesville (1968), 41–43.

[49] *Peter H. Sand*, Roman Origins of the Ethiopian "Law of the Kings" (Fetha Negast), Excerpt from a book available at: https://www.researchgate.net/publication/292976869_

Formally issued laws started to play some role in the country only as late as the beginning of the twentieth century[50]. In the pre-World War II period, rudimental steps were taken in the direction of the development of substantive law. That said, by mid-1950s the laws of Ethiopia were still an amorphous mix of statutes and decrees mostly focusing on the field of public law. Social and civil matters were governed mainly by the traditions and customs of the various ethnic and religious groups[51]. No commercial laws of note existed. Prof. Jean Escarra, who mostly drafted the 1960 Commercial Code, conducted an inventory of existing commercial laws and business practices before embarking on the drafting project. He concluded that by mid-1950s the available texts were irregular collections and that it was not always easy to tell whether they were draft proposals or formally passed laws. Besides, it was very difficult to know if they were enforced effectively in practice[52].

The legal system of Ethiopia underwent drastic changes in the years following the end of the Second World War. Particularly, the way laws were conceived, issued, communicated and implemented changed markedly in comparison to the eras preceding that. The Ethiopian State was increasingly modernized as far as legal development is concerned during these years[53]. Among other things, Ethiopia undertook the codification of its laws in the decade between 1955 and 1965. Six codes that can be regarded as such in the fullest sense of the term were promulgated. The 1960 Commercial Code drafted by two French professors was one of them. Prof. Jean Escarra, professor of comparative commercial law at the University of Paris was tasked with the drafting of the Commercial Code[54]. He died after drafting the bulk of three of the five books that constitute the 1960 Commercial Code. Hence, Prof. Alfred Jauffret, another French Professor, finalized the drafting work[55].

Roman_Origins_of_the_Ethiopian_Law_of_the_Kings_Fetha_Negast, last visited on 10th July 2025.

50 *Jacques Vanderlinden*, Civil Law Common Law Influences on the Developing Law of Ethiopia, 16 Buffalo Law Review (1967), 252.

51 *John Beckstrom*, Transplantation of Legal Systems: An Early Report on the Reception of Western Laws in Ethiopia, 21 American Journal of Comparative Law (1973), 559.

52 *Peter Winship* (ed.), Background Documents of the Ethiopian Commercial Code of 1960, Haileselassie I University (1974), 14.

53 *Norman Singer*, Modernization of Law in Ethiopia, 76 Harvard International Law Journal (1970), 79.

54 *John Beckstrom*, JH Transplantation of Legal Systems: An Early Report on the Reception of Western Laws in Ethiopia, 21 American Journal of Comparative Law (1973), 559. Prof. Escarra died before he could complete the drafting work. Hence Prof. Jauffret of the University of Paris had to complete the drafting of the 1960 Commercial Code of Ethiopia.

55 Position of the Business Community on the Revision of the Commercial Code of Ethiopia, Document prepared by the Addis Ababa Chamber of Commerce and Sectoral Associations in collaboration with Swedish Agency for International Development Cooperation (2008), 7.

The new codes did not have much Ethiopian content. Pre-existing laws were repealed in some cases explicitly and in others by implication. As for the customs of the country, there was not much for the drafters to rely upon because no systematic survey of the existing customs had been conducted[56]. This was particularly the case as far as commercial laws were concerned. So, overall, it is safe to conclude that the content of the laws, especially of those that pertain to commerce, is essentially foreign. This raises the question of which foreign sources were used and their contribution.

As regards the system from which the borrowing took place, we see that the substantive laws by and large followed Romano-Germanic legal principles. In drafting the Civil Code, for instance, French law had the most extensive impact, though the laws of many other jurisdictions were consulted[57]. Prof. Escarra, states that he was instructed by the Ethiopian Codification Commission to base the Commercial Code on continental European doctrines[58]. All the same, he goes to great lengths to emphasize the dangers inherent in reproducing the laws of any single jurisdiction and that he would consult even the laws of common law jurisdictions[59]. That being said, the structure and content of the code, especially Book I, dealing with general commercial law shows that French commercial law exerted the biggest influence. We note, perhaps because of that, a striking parallel between the topics covered, structure and organization of the OHADA rules on General Commercial Law and Book I of the 1960 Commercial Code.

2. *Conceptual and Structural Similarities*

Book I of the OHADA Uniform Act on General Commercial Law, for instance, is titled "the status of a trader" and begins by defining traders and commercial transactions[60]. It then goes on to determine the persons that have the "capacity to trade and deals with minors, spouses of traders and people who may be prohibited from engaging in trade by law or the court"[61]. Similarly, the 1960 Commercial Code starts off by defining traders, in terms of certain transactions that it deems are commercial[62]. It then proceeds to regulate the capacity to trade. It

---

[56] *Beckstrom* (n. 51), 559–560.

[57] *Singer* (n. 53), 88–89.

[58] *Winship* (n. 52), 12.

[59] *Winship* (n. 52), 29.

[60] OHADA Uniform Act relating to General Commercial Law, adopted on 17th April 1997, Articles 2–4.

[61] OHADA Uniform Act (n. 60), Articles 6, 7, and 8.

[62] Commercial Code of the Empire of Ethiopia Proclamation No.166/1960, Articles 5 and 10.

deals, particularly, with the spouse of traders, minors and persons who are incapable of carrying on trade under civil law[63].

Understandably, the detailed rules are not always identical. For instance, the Commercial Code of Ethiopia contains nothing comparable to the OHADA rule that prohibits civil servants, employees of state-owned enterprises, lawyers and certified public accounts from concurrently carrying on trade[64].

Yet another conceptual similarity between the two is that they both dedicate dozens of provisions to *fonds de commerce*, a distinctive feature of French commercial law[65]. The concept of *fonds de commerce* which under French law denotes "all the movable goods, whether tangible or intangible, which are used by the trader in operating a commercial activity, and which have the purpose of attracting his customers" is dealt with under the 1960 Commercial Code[66]. The 1960 Commercial Code provides more or less the same definition of the notion which it translates as "business". It reads, "[a] business is an incorporeal movable consisting of all movable property brought together and organized for the purpose of carrying out any of the commercial activities specified in Article 5 of this Code"[67]. It then emphatically states that a business mainly consists of goodwill and lists other possible incorporeal elements of business such as tradename under which business is carried out, and the right to lease premises in which the trade is carried out[68].

The OHADA Act provides essentially the same definition. It states that business consists of all the movable things, tangible and intangible, that enable a trader to attract and maintain customers[69]. It emphasizes that goodwill and trade sign or trade name are the central elements of business and goes on to regulate the management and transfer of a business[70]. The Commercial Code of Ethiopia dedicates a total of 86 Articles to business, particularly its elements, and transactions in business such as sale, mortgage and hire of a business[71]. The parallel between the two laws does not end with the notion of business though. Similarly, the OHADA Uniform Act dedicates several articles to "commercial intermediaries", while the Commercial Code regulates comparable persons which it calls "auxiliaries and agents"[72]. There are also other similarities such as

[63] Commercial Code of the Empire of Ethiopia (n. 62), Articles 11–27.

[64] OHADA Uniform Act relating to General Commercial Law (n. 60), Article 9.

[65] OHADA Uniform Act relating to General Commercial Law (n. 60), Articles 103–136 and the 1960 Commercial Code of Ethiopia (n. 63), Articles 124–209.

[66] *Belew Yazachew*, The Sale of a Business as a Going Concern under the Ethiopian Commercial Code: A Commentary, 24(2) Journal of Ethiopian Law (2010), 92.

[67] Commercial Code of the Empire of Ethiopia (n. 62), Article 124.

[68] Commercial Code of 1960 (n. 62), Article 127.

[69] OHADA Uniform Act relating to General Commercial Law (n. 60), Article 103.

[70] OHADA Uniform Act relating to General Commercial Law (n. 60), Articles 104–136.

[71] Commercial Code of the Empire of Ethiopia (n. 62), Articles 124–209.

[72] OHADA Uniform Act relating to General Commercial Law (n. 60), Articles 137–159, and Commercial Code of the Empire of Ethiopia (n. 62), Articles 28–62.

regarding the rules on books and accounts that the trader should keep and detailed rules on commercial registration into which we need not delve here. The bottom line is that the OHADA Uniform Act relating to General Commercial Law and Book I of the 1960 Commercial Code of Ethiopia are alike at both conceptual and structural level – a testament to their kinship.

3. The Rationales for the Choice of the OHADA Uniform Act

The Ethiopian Government had been making an effort to revise the 1960 Commercial Code on and off since late 1980s. A Working Group on the Commercial Code was formed by the Advisory Council in January 2019 to jump-start the sluggishly proceeding revision of the Commercial Code and the author had the privilege of leading and coordinating the revision effort[73]. The Advisory Council presented policy recommendations regarding the revision of the Commercial Code to the Council of Ministers in February 2019. It underscored that trade and investment have increasingly taken transnational character owing to advances in technology and communications which have made the world into a single globalized village. In view of this, the Advisory Council emphasized the need for considering foreign commercial practices and legal developments to accommodate the needs and expectations of foreign investors in order to make Ethiopia a competitive investment destination. OHADA Uniform Acts were among the foreign laws chosen for benchmarking owing to the following reasons.

a) Ethiopian jurists look to continental legal sources, especially French law, for authority when confronted with new legal issues of commercial nature owing to the conceptual and structural similarities discussed in the previous section. This is natural because diffusion is generally driven "by the emulation of others who are perceived as fundamentally similar and who are hence perceived to be facing the same problems"[74]. The problem is that hardly any lawyer, who is well versed in Ethiopian commercial law, is also fluent in French or other continental European languages and able to understand legal texts written in them. Besides, material from civil-law countries is not easily accessible. This makes it very difficult to follow developments in French and other continental laws. Since OHADA Acts are available in English, benchmarking them was a way of peeping into continental European law, especially French law. The shared French origins of the 1960 Commercial Code and the OHADA Acts was a major consideration, in other words.

---

[73] Report of the Working Group on the Commercial Code of Ethiopia, dated 11th January 2019, available on file with the author.

[74] *Holger Spamann* (2009) Contemporary Legal Transplants – Legal Families and the Diffusion of (corporate) Law, Harvard, John M. Olin Center for Law, Economics, and Business, Discussion Paper No. 28, 46–47, available at SSRN: https://ssrn.com/abstract=1411704.

b) The OHADA Uniform Acts were adopted about four decades after the 1960 Commercial Code of Ethiopia. The OHADA Uniform Acts relating to General Commercial Law were, in particular, adopted in 1997. So, benchmarking them was seen as a way of keeping up with current changes in the shared parent system of laws in Europe, especially in France.

c) It was expected that OHADA member countries would customize continental European commercial law to the institutional and economic context of African countries at comparable levels of development to Ethiopia. This was yet another reason for benchmarking the OHADA laws in the revision of the Commercial Code of Ethiopia.

VII. Extent of Borrowing from the OHADA Rules and the Limits to that

In what follows we look at the extent to which the OHADA Uniform Act relating to General Commercial Law impacted the revision of Book I of the Commercial Code of Ethiopia. Besides, we raise some of the reasons that limited the level of borrowing rules.

1. The Definition of Traders

Professor Escarra, who had started drafting the 1960 Commercial Code, raises the question of whether a commercial code should apply only as among traders or to certain acts that are deemed to be acts of commerce, irrespective of who carries them out. He indicates that there are two major approaches depending on how the question is answered: the subjective and objective approach. Commercial law applies, according to the subjective approach, to a group of people defined as traders. In contrast, it applies to acts of commerce irrespective of the actors carrying out the activity according to the objective approach[75]. He affirmed that there is hardly any law that follows purely one or the other of the two approaches but chose to take the subjective approach as a point of departure for the 1960 Commercial Code of Ethiopia. Professor Alfred Jauffret, who finalized the drafting work, chose to stick to the subjective approach chosen by his predecessor[76].

The 1960 Commercial Code, based on the foregoing choice of approach, defines "traders" as persons who "professionally and for gain carry on any of" the twenty-one activities that it lists[77]. Neither the *chapeaux* of Article 5 nor any-

[75] *Winship* (n. 52), 34.
[76] *Winship* (n. 52), 34–35.
[77] Commercial Code of the Empire of Ethiopia (n. 62), Article 5.

thing in the list itself indicates that the list was meant to be illustrative. In fact, Professor Jauffret clearly indicates in his report of 1st March 1958, that he tried to provide a list that is as complete as possible of the activities carried out by traders and hence decided that the enumeration be limitative, rather than illustrative[78].

The limitative approach did not seem to pose difficulties in the initial years. Ethiopia of the 1960s was essentially a feudal society characterized by subsistence farming and limited export of primary commodities like coffee. Not much was going on in terms of industrialization or trade in goods and services[79]. To make matters worse, the Commercial Code was rendered practically irrelevant between 1974 and 1991 owing to the 1974 Socialist Revolution that nationalized all commercial and industrial firms of note and left little to no room for private business initiatives[80].

The exhaustive list under Article 5 proved problematic only after the adoption of the 1992 Policy Framework Papers that re-introduced free market economy based on the agreement reached between the newly installed government on the one hand and the International Monetary Fund and the World Bank on the other[81]. Entrepreneurs wanted to establish schools, colleges, hospitals and provide consultancy services of all sorts for profit. The problem was that these activities do not appear among the twenty-one commercial activities enumerated under Article 5 of the 1960 Commercial Code. The understanding of government officials in charge of commercial registration and issuance of business licenses was that engaging in activities that did not appear on the list was prohibited. Owing to recurrent complaints of entrepreneurs faced with this problem a proclamation was issued that maintained the limitative nature of the definition but provided for the possibility of the Council of Ministers, through regulations, to add new commercial activities to the list[82]. An appendix was added to the proclamation that included new activities such as the establishment of colleges and hospitals to the list of commercial activities in respect of which business licenses may be issued[83]. This proved to be a short-lived solution. Commercial activities that had not been anticipated by the new proclamation started to emerge just a couple of years later thanks to advances in technology such as the internet.

---

78 *Winship* (n. 52), 50.

79 *Chole Eshetu*, Running to Keep in the Same Place: Industrialization 1941–1974, in: Shiferaw Bekele (ed.), An Economic History of Ethiopia: The Imperial Era 1941–1974, OSSREA (1995), 195.

80 *Chole Eshetu*, Underdevelopment in Ethiopia, OSSREA, Addis Abada (2004), 100–101.

81 *Eshetu* (n. 80), 117–123.

82 Commercial Registration and Business Licensing Proclamation No. 67/1997, Article 2(2).

83 Commercial Registration Proclamation No. 67/1997, item 5 and 6 of the Appendix.

It is in the foregoing context that the Commercial Code was revised in 2021. The team entrusted with the revision of Book I of the Commercial Code proposed a change in approach along the lines of OHADA Uniform Act relating to General Commercial Law. Article 2 of the OHADA Uniform Act defines traders as "persons whose usual occupation is to carry out commercial transactions" while Article 3 goes on to state "commercial transactions shall *include* in particular [emphasis added by the author]" and then goes on to give examples[84]. In short, the approach to the definition of traders under the OHADA Uniform Act is illustrative rather than limitative. The OHADA approach was seen as the better one because it did not arrest progress by forcing entrepreneurs to move at the pace of government's law-making speed. The justification given was that the law should assume freedom to pursue any economic activity for profit in so far as it is not prohibited by law. This is compatible with the principle espoused by the Civil Code provision which states "every person is free to exercise any activity which he deems proper in that which concerns his calling and leisure"[85]. We note at this juncture that the Commercial Code itself states that the Civil Code provisions apply "to the status and activities of persons and business organizations carrying on trade unless otherwise provided" by it[86].

In sum, the Revised Commercial Code adopted OHADA's subjective, illustrative approach and reads, in the relevant part: "[p]ersons who professionally and for gain carry on *any of the following or similar activities* shall be deemed to be traders [emphasis added by the author]"[87]. But it goes on to list some 37 activities including activities that are listed neither under OHADA Uniform Act nor the 1960 Commercial Code. These include recycling waste, veterinary and human health services, office support, computer and software related services, fitness and beauty establishments, operating trade fairs, consultancy services including auditing, security and even funeral services[88].

The idea was to include as many economic activities as possible to minimize the risk of people being denied license to engage in activities of their choice, given the proclivity of the Ethiopian bureaucracy to deny whatever is not expressly authorized by the law. We note at this juncture that nothing in the revised Commercial Code Proclamation No. 1243/2021 excludes the possibility of relevant authorities issuing detailed licensing requirements and professional standard of conduct where the nature of the activity included under Article 5 calls for that.

---

[84] Uniform Act relating to General Commercial Law (n. 60), Articles 2 and 3.

[85] Civil Code of the Empire of Ethiopia Proclamation No. 165.1960, Article 16(1).

[86] Commercial Code of the Empire of Ethiopia (n. 62), Article 1.

[87] Commercial Code Proclamation 1243/2021, Article 5.

[88] Compare Commercial Code of the Empire of Ethiopia Proclamation of 2021, Federal Negarit Gazette Extraordinary Issue No. 1243/2021, Article 5 with OHADA Uniform Act relating to General Commercial Law (n. 60), Article 3.

2. Commercial Lease of Premises

The OHADA Uniform Act relating to General Commercial Law provides a comprehensive framework for commercial leases under Articles 69–101. These provisions govern the formation, duration, renewal and termination of lease of premises or buildings used for commercial, industrial, handcraft or professional purposes[89]. The provisions governing lease apply to corporate persons too irrespective of whether they are lessors or lessees[90].

Though the 1960 Commercial Code of Ethiopia likewise contains provisions on commercial lease it leaves most matters to the Civil Code[91]. It provides essentially only two protections to the lessee trader. The first is the protection it grants to the trader against unfair competition by the lessor. Particularly, the law prohibits the lessor, once the lease agreement is concluded, from carrying out a trade similar to that carried out by the lessee in the same building[92]. Besides the law regards as invalid any contractual term in the lease agreement that prevents the lessee from assigning the contract of lease or from sub-letting the premises to the person who buys his business. Likewise, any contractual term which makes an assignment of lease right subject to the consent of the lessor is of no effect[93]. These are the deviations which the 1960 Commercial Code makes from the rules under the Civil Code of Ethiopia[94].

The Revised Commercial Code 1243/2021 has maintained the foregoing two safeguards accorded to a trader in relation to the lease of premises in which he carries out business. It protects a lessee trader from unfair competition by the lessor by prohibiting the latter from carrying on a trade similar to that carried out by the lessee in the same building[95]. It also outlaws any contractual provision which either prohibits or makes subject to the consent of the lessor, assignment of lease right or sub-letting by the lessee trader[96]. With respect to assignment of lease and sub-letting, Ethiopian law affords the trader stronger protection than that accorded under OHADA Act Articles 86–90. Under OHADA, any partial or total sub-lease by a trader is prohibited unless otherwise stipulated in the lease agreement between the trader and lessor. Even where sub-lease is so authorized the lessee must notify the lessor under pain of nullity of the sub-

[89] OHADA UA on GCL (n. 60), Article 69.

[90] OHADA UA on GCL (n. 60), Article 70.

[91] Commercial Code of the Empire of Ethiopia (n. 62), Article 142; Civil Code of Ethiopia Proclamation 165/1960, Articles 2896–2965.

[92] Commercial Code of the Empire of Ethiopia Proclamation (n. 62), Article 144.

[93] Commercial Code of the Empire of Ethiopia Proclamation (n. 62), Article 145.

[94] Civil Code of the Empire of Ethiopia Proclamation (n. 85), Article 2959.

[95] Commercial Code Proclamation of 2021 (n. 88), Article 118.

[96] Commercial Code Proclamation of 2021 (n. 88), Article 119.

lease[97]. So, with respect to these two issues the OHADA rules were not considered to offer something of value in the Ethiopian context.

The OHADA Act does, however, vest in a lessee trader, a very important right of renewal of the lease agreement, irrespective of whether the lease agreement was for a specified or unspecified duration. The lessee only has to establish that he carried out the activity provided for in the lease agreement in the leased premises for at least two years in accordance with the conditions stipulated in the lease agreement[98]. The lessor may object to the renewal of the lease by paying an eviction indemnity in the amount agreed by the parties, or to be determined by a court, in the absence of an agreement on the matter[99]. Good and proper grounds on which the lessor may refuse to renew the lease without paying an eviction indemnity have been enumerated in the law. They include failure on the part of the lessee to fulfil a substantial obligation under the lease and intention on the part of the lessor to demolish and rebuild the structure in which the premises rented are located[100]. Unfortunately, neither the revised Commercial Code Proclamation No 1243/2021 nor the Civil Code provisions that complement it give a comparable protection of the right to the renewal of the lease agreement. Under Ethiopian law a contract of lease made for a fixed period terminates "as of right on the expiration of the period agreed upon without the necessity of giving notice"[101].

The provisions of the OHADA Act granting a trader the right to renewal of the lease enable a trader to pursue long-term business strategies as he will have no fear of being forced to leave premises after developing a clientele. The absence of similar rules in Ethiopia enables unscrupulous property owners to engage in unfair practice. They lease property to start-ups to only evict them once the latter develop a clientele and then either run the same business in the property or lease the property to others at a much higher rent.

The inclusion of rules that entitle a trader to the renewal of the lease agreement along the lines of OHADA Uniform Act was discussed. Experts involved in the revision process were mostly convinced of the merits of the proposal but were afraid this would engender serious opposition by property owners significantly delaying or even derailing the revision process that had been proceeding on and off sluggishly for three decades[102]. Besides, the absence of meaningful

---

97 OHADA UA on GCL (n. 60), Article 89.

98 OHADA UA on GCL (n. 60), Article 91.

99 OHADA UA on GCL (n. 60), Article 94.

100 OHADA UA on GCL (n. 60), Article 95.

101 Commercial Code of 2021 (n. 88), Article 116 cum Civil Code Proclamation (n. 85), Article 2965.

102 The Author, who led and coordinated the revision of the Commercial Code discussed the matter at the time with Mr. Yazachew Below who was coordinating the revision effort on Book I of the 1960 Commercial Code in which these provisions are found. According to Mr. Yazachew Below, this is why the Committee decided to stick to the old rules.

commentaries in English on the pertinent OHADA rules and the inaccessibility of the jurisprudence of the Common Court of Justice and Arbitration (CCJA) on these and other rules limited the extent of borrowing from the OHADA Act.

3. Commercial Sales

Book V of the OHADA Uniform Act (Articles 202–288) is dedicated to commercial sales of goods between traders[103]. The provisions in this book do not apply to sales to consumers, sales by order of the court, sale by auction and sales of securities, stocks, currency, and the assignment of debt[104]. Likewise, the provisions of the book do not apply to "contracts in which the major part of the obligation of a party that supplies the goods consists in the supply of labour or other services"[105].

The provisions under Book V of the OHADA Act deal with, among others, the creation of a sales contract (Articles 210–218), obligations of the parties to the contract of sale (Articles 219–244), penalties for breach of contract (Articles 245–282) and effects of the contract (Articles 283–288).

The 1960 Commercial Code did not contain comparable provisions on the sale of goods as between traders. This was left to part of the Civil Code of Ethiopia that is dedicated to special contracts. Articles 2266–2402 of the Civil Code regulate the sale of "corporeal chattels"[106]. The 1960 Commercial Code incorporated these provisions by stating "[...] the provisions of the Civil Code shall apply to the status and activities of persons and business organizations carrying on trade" in the absence of a contrary provision in the Commercial Code[107]. The team that worked on the revision of Book I of the Commercial Code was of the opinion that this approach should be maintained and changes to particular rules on special sale be considered when the Civil Code is revised, which was expected to begin soon at the time[108].

VIII. Conclusions

We considered in this contribution the actual and likely impact of OHADA's Uniform Acts in non-Francophone Africa in the context of the recently

[103] OHADA UA on GCL (n. 60), Article 202.
[104] OHADA UA on GCL (n. 60), Article 203.
[105] OHADA UA on GCL (n. 60), Article 204.
[106] Civil Code of the Empire of Ethiopia Proclamation (n. 85), Article 2267.
[107] Commercial Code of the Empire of Ethiopia Proclamation (n. 62).
[108] Exchange with Mr. Yazachew Below, coordinator and member of the team of experts that worked on the revision of Book I of the Commercial Code of Ethiopia, 11th March 2025.

launched African Continental Free Trade Area (AfCFTA). Particularly, we took Ethiopia as a case study focusing on the role the OHADA Uniform Act Relating to General Commercial Law played in the revision of the Commercial Code of Ethiopia.

We find that the OHADA Uniform Acts are already in force in Guinea-Bissau and Equatorial Guinea, countries that speak Portuguese and Spanish respectively. Besides, the fact that OHADA Acts have the full force of law in seventeen of the fifty-four African countries that have recently launched the African Continental Free Trade Area gives them the first-mover advantage in the harmonization of commercial laws that may take place under the auspices of AfCFTA.

OHADA Uniform Acts are also well placed to influence legal reforms that take place at the initiative of individual African countries because most African countries either fully follow the Civil Law tradition or a mix of Civil Law- and Islamic/Common Law traditions. In the case of Ethiopia where all substantive laws are modelled after continental European Legal System, particularly French law, the OHADA Acts are taken as one of the natural comparators in legal reform process. The OHADA Uniform Act Relating to General Commercial Law was, for example, taken as a benchmark for the revision of Book I of the Commercial Code in 2021. The definition of traders, which is a core concept in the first book of the code was reformed along the lines of Articles 2 and 3 of the OHADA Act.

That said, the absence of meaningful commentaries in English on the OHADA rules, the inaccessibility of the jurisprudence of the Common Court of Justice and Arbitration (CCJA) and the fear of serious opposition potentially derailing the revision process limited the extent of borrowing some of the rules from the Uniform Act.

The Stakes of Commercial Dispute Resolution in OHADA and EU Legal Frameworks

Nestor Kouami

I. Introduction

The globalization of international trade has prompted regional and sub-regional organizations to adapt to the various challenges related to legal and judicial security in business law. Indeed, regional and sub-regional organizations such as the European Union, the African Union (with the AfCFTA), and the Organization for the Harmonization of Business Law in Africa (OHADA) have modernized their commercial dispute resolution mechanisms in order to reassure investors.

These regional and sub-regional organizations have thus adapted both judicial procedures in commercial matters and alternative dispute resolution (ADR) methods such as arbitration and mediation to the needs of commercial exchanges. This primarily concerns trade between member states of the same regional or sub-regional organization. This is the case with the European Union, the African Union (through the AfCFTA), and OHADA.

It is important to note, however, that these actors have gone even further by establishing trade agreements with third-party states. One example is the Lugano Convention, concluded between the European Union and third states, notably Switzerland.

In order to secure the business law environment and facilitate trade within their respective territories, the signatory states of the Lugano Convention and the OHADA member states have implemented innovative legal, judicial, and extra-judicial instruments. These include the various OHADA Uniform Acts[1] and the mechanisms under the Lugano Convention designed for the settlement of commercial disputes[2]. The AfCFTA will not be addressed within the scope of our analysis.

[1] These include Uniform Acts on security interests, collective proceedings, enforcement, commercial companies, arbitration, mediation, general commercial law, etc.

[2] CJEU, Case C-343/22, 15 May 2023, PT v VB, note *Mélin F./Hartley T. C.*, in: Hartley (ed.), Choice-of-court agreements under the European and International Instruments: The Revised Brussels I Regulation, the Lugano Convention, and the Hague Convention, Oxford 2013, p. 332.

However, it must be emphasized that although the dispute resolution mechanisms introduced by the Lugano Convention and OHADA are innovative, they do not achieve the same level of effectiveness. This disparity is at the heart of our article and leads us to the following question:

Would a comparative study of the effectiveness and weaknesses of the various commercial dispute resolution instruments in the two community systems not be useful in order to adapt them to the new demands of international trade?

To answer this question, it will be necessary to present a brief overview of the legal and judicial frameworks applicable to commercial disputes within the OHADA and European Union[3] areas.

The purpose of this article is to provide a brief overview of the legal and judicial frameworks applicable to commercial disputes in OHADA and EU areas and to identify, in the form of recommendations, efficient models to be taken into account in the drafting of a European Business Code.

Part I therefore deals with the mechanisms for settling commercial disputes in OHADA and EU areas. Part II is dedicated to the framework for implementing alternative dispute resolution methods.

1. Mechanisms in force in the OHADA and EU Areas

a) The case of EU member states

Within the framework of regional cooperation between the EU and the States of the European Free Trade Association (EFTA), we have been able to identify the Lugano Convention of 1988, revised in 2007. This convention facilitates the resolution of commercial disputes before the courts of the States bound by this convention. It also facilitates the circulation and enforcement of judicial decisions such as debt recovery in commercial matters on the territory of the States bound by this convention. The Convention applies to commercial contracts, the insurance sector, commercial leases, rights in rem in immovable property, etc.

Secondly, there are several relevant regulations, such as Regulation (EU) No 1215/2012 of the European Parliament and of the Council of 12th December 2012 on jurisdiction and the recognition and enforcement of judgments in civil and commercial matters (Brussels I bis). This act contains rules on the determination of the place of jurisdiction and on the recognition and enforcement of judgments.

The aim of Regulation (EC) No 805/2004 of the European Parliament and the Council of 21st April 2004 creating a European Enforcement Order for uncontested claims is to facilitate the recovery of claims that are certain, liquid, and due.

---

[3] Including the legal effects of the Lugano Convention.

The Council Regulation (EC) No 1206/2001 of 28th May 2001 on cooperation between the judicial authorities of the Member States in the taking of evidence in civil or commercial matters improves the circulation of evidence between the courts of the Member States.

Council Decision (EC) No 470/2001 of 28th May 2001 establishing a European Judicial Network in civil and commercial matters facilitates interaction between the courts of the member states.

Regulation (EC) No 1393/2007 of the European Parliament and of the Council of 13th November 2007 on the service in the Member States of judicial and extrajudicial documents in civil or commercial matters facilitates the administration of justice in the Member States.

The Regulation (EU) 2015/848 of the European Parliament and of the Council of 20th May 2015 on insolvency proceedings fosters the legal and judicial supervision of undertakings in difficulty.

The Regulation (EC) No 861/2007 of the European Parliament and of the Council of 11th July 2007 establishes a European Small Claims Procedure for the settlement of cross-border small claims in civil or commercial matters with a monetary value of up to € 5,000.

The Regulation (EC) No 593/2008 of the European Parliament and of the Council of 17th June 2008 on the law applicable to contractual obligations (Rome I) covers conflict of laws and contractual obligations in civil and commercial matters.

And lastly, Regulation (EC) No 1896/2006 of the European Parliament and of the Council of 12th December 2006 creates a European order for payment procedure.

What about the OHADA regional mechanism for the settlement of commercial disputes?

2. Within OHADA Area

With reference to Article 13 of the OHADA Treaty, "disputes relating to the application of Uniform Acts shall be settled at first instance and on appeal by the courts of the Contracting States". The national courts of the Contracting States are classified as ordinary courts under OHADA law. The CCJA acts as a supreme regional court without referral. Furthermore, in an opinion of 30th April 2001, the CCJA clarified the supranational scope of the OHADA Uniform Acts on the national law of the States[4].

[4] CCJA n° 001/2001/EP; *Sehonnoudéa J.* A., Réflexion sur l'ordre public en droit public OHADA, Thèse de Doctorat Université Panthéon Assas, 2024.

The limitation period for commercial sales is set at two years[5]. This limitation period for commercial sales expires on the date on which the guarantee is fulfilled (see Article 276 UA GCL).

The time limit for lodging a challenge (e.g. release) with the competent court in the context of a debt attachment procedure is one month[6].

Where the creditor provides proof of the existence of a claim and demonstrates that there is a risk of recovery, he may apply to the competent court for authorisation to carry out a protective attachment. This protective attachment may relate to any tangible or intangible movable property belonging to the debtor[7]. If the creditor has an enforceable title, he will not need the judge's authorisation to carry out a protective attachment[8].

Attention should also be paid to the Common Court of Justice and Arbitration whose main role is to unify case law with regard to the provisions of the CCJA Rules of Procedure revised in Ouagadougou at the OHADA Council of Ministers on 30th and 31st January 2014.

The CCJA is the supreme regional court. This is illustrated in the case of *Monsieur Lamory Sanogo v Côte d'Ivoire Telecom*[9], in which the CCJA was asked to give an opinion in the context of the application of OHADA treaties or uniform acts, particularly in commercial matters[10]. There are two types of appeals against decisions of the CCJA in commercial matters. The first is third-party proceedings[11].

This is a request made by a third party to obtain the retraction or reformulation of a CCJA decision that is prejudicial to him or her. The second is revision[12]. This requires the existence of a new fact unknown to the parties and the Court that could have influenced the course of the judgment if the CCJA had been aware of it.

Offences relating to commercial matters, commercial companies and securities fall within the jurisdiction of national courts[13].

---

[5] Article 274 UA on General Commercial Law; *Lelo di Makungu U./Bosakelia Lokwa J./Bkomito Gambu J.*, Traité de droit commercial OHADA, 2022, p. 5–326.

[6] Article 170 UA on Simplified Procedures and Enforcement Measures (AUPSVE); *Agossadou J. S./Dogue K. O.*, OHADA: Droit et pratique du recouvrement et des voies d'exécution, 2024, p. 10–720.

[7] Article 54 AUPSVE; ibid.

[8] Article 55 AUPSVE; ibid.

[9] CCJA n° 018/2010 of 25th March 2010; ibid.

[10] Articles 14 and 15 revised OHADA Treaty; ibid, note 5.

[11] Article 47 CCJA Rules; ibid.

[12] Article 49 CCJA Rules; *Ndzuenkeu A.*, Un nouveau Règlement intérieur pour redynamiser la CCJA, 2024, p. 3–7.

[13] Articles 69 and 140 Uniform Act relating to General Commercial Law (AUDCG); Articles 886–905 of the Revised Uniform Act relating to the Law on Commercial Companies and Economic Interest Groupings (AUDSGIE); Op. cit, note n°5.

Under Article 14(5) of the OHADA Treaty, the CCJA has the power of evocation. It can give final rulings on the merits as an appeal court or as the highest court in a commercial case. In this case, the CCJA replaces the national courts of the member states.

In OHADA law, we have a unification of case law in all specific commercial matters at regional level with short processing times adapted to the speed requirements of the business world. Cases may be referred to the CCJA either as a court of first instance or as a court of appeal. The decisions of the CCJA in commercial matters are directly applicable in the member states.

We can conclude for this first part that: In the context of the application of the Lugano Convention, the question of the simplification of procedures in commercial matters remains unresolved, even if this Convention constitutes a step forward. Within the OHADA area, there is a regional court for commercial matters with jurisdiction to ensure uniform application of the uniform acts in commercial disputes. The operation of the CCJA in commercial matters may be taken as an example in context of the implementation of the European Business Code.

The European Union may draw inspiration from the OHADA model in uniform acts in commercial matters, regional judicial procedures, judicial cooperation between national judges and the CCJA judge in commercial matters in order to better tailor its own law to the real needs of economic operators.

However, it should be noted that economic operators tend to avoid complex commercial legal proceedings in favour of alternative dispute resolution methods. These include arbitration and mediation.

III. The Framework for Alternative Dispute Resolution (Arbitration and Mediation)

1. Arbitration in OHADA and EU Law

a) Arbitration in the OHADA

We have two categories of arbitration: institutional arbitration and ad hoc arbitration. Institutional arbitration is governed by the CCJA Arbitration Rules of 23rd November 2017 and the revised OHADA Treaty of 17th October 2008. Ad hoc arbitration is governed by common Community law: the Uniform Act on Arbitration of 23rd November 2017 and the national texts of the Member States.

aa) Institutional Arbitration under OHADA Law

CCJA institutional arbitration is governed by the Arbitration Rules (A.R.), the Procedural Rules (P.R.) of the CCJA and the Uniform Act on Arbitration

(UAA). The contract from which the arbitration dispute arises must have a link (place of performance, domicile of the parties, place of conclusion of the contract, etc.) with a State party to OHADA[14].

Regular arbitration proceedings before the CCJA arbitral tribunal must meet the following requirements: Request for arbitration by the parties[15], existence and validity of the arbitration agreement[16], proper composition of the arbitral tribunal (appointment and confirmation of arbitrators)[17], removal or replacement of arbitrators[18], and proper conduct of the arbitration proceedings[19]. The CCJA arbitral tribunal issues a draft award signed by the arbitrators. This draft award is sent to the Secretary General of the CCJA for formal validation after review[20]. Once the award has been validated, it becomes final.

The CCJA has jurisdiction to hear appeals challenging the validity of arbitral awards[21], third-party proceedings[22], and the granting of regional exequatur for the recognition and enforcement of arbitral awards[23].

The parties may choose an arbitration centre located in an OHADA member state[24]. In this case, the local courts act as judges of the annulment, recognition and enforcement of arbitral awards. The CCJA acts only as the supreme regional court for decisions of national courts.

Furthermore, ad hoc arbitration in the OHADA area is not exempt from the standards of uniform law.

bb) Ad hoc Arbitration where the Law Applied to the Substance of the Dispute is OHADA Law

Ad hoc arbitration is governed by the Uniform Act on Arbitration (UAA) and the national law (Code of Civil Procedure) of the member states. Where the seat of the ad hoc arbitral tribunal is located in a state outside the OHADA area, the parties may not choose OHADA law as the law applicable to the substance of

---

[14] Article 21 revised OHADA treaty and Article 2.1 CCJA R.A.; *Fénéon A./Tchakoua J.-M.*, Le nouveau droit de l'arbitrage et de la médiation en Afrique (Ohada), 2024, p. 10–480.

[15] Article 5 CCJA A.R.; *Ndiaye Mbaye M.*, L'arbitrage OHADA en questions et réponses, 2024, p. 5–65.

[16] Articles 9 and 10 CCJA A.R.; ibid.

[17] Article 3 CCJA A.R.; ibid.

[18] Article 4 CCJA A.R.; ibid.

[19] Article 4 CCJA A.R.; ibid.

[20] Article 23 CCJA A.R.; *Darly-Aymar D.*, Panorama de la jurisprudence de la Cour commune de justice et d'arbitrage en droit de l'arbitrage: années 2021 et 2022, Cahiers de l'arbitrage – *n°*2, 2023, p. 363 et seq.

[21] Article 29 CCJA A.R.; ibid.

[22] Article 33 CCJA A.R.; ibid.

[23] Article 30 CCJA A.R.; ibid.

[24] Article 10(1) UAA.; ibid.

the dispute[25]. In the context of this type of ad hoc arbitration, the parties are free to choose the rules of procedure in the arbitration[26].

The various phases of OHADA institutional and ad hoc arbitration are governed by unified regional legislation. This creates an environment of legal and judicial certitude for investors. In addition, investors have the guarantees they need to recover their claims through the compulsory enforcement of arbitration awards. One example is the validity of regional authorisation execution (exequatur) in all OHADA Member States.

In light of the above, we note that arbitration law is firmly anchored in the OHADA area. Compared to the European Union area, there are certain specific features to highlight.

b) Arbitration in the EU

aa) Exclusion of Arbitration from the Scope of the Brussels I bis Regulation

As arbitration is excluded by Regulation (EU) n 1215/2012 Brussels I bis, the recognition and the enforcement of domestic and international arbitral awards are governed by the national law of the Member States[27]. This also applies to any action or ancillary proceedings relating to arbitration such as the establishment of an arbitral tribunal or the powers of arbitrators. Member States may refer to the 1958 New York Convention on the Recognition and Enforcement of Foreign Arbitral Awards and to their national laws when implementing procedures for the recognition and enforcement of international arbitral awards[28].

If a court of a Member State has been seized of an action in a matter in respect of which the parties have entered into an arbitration agreement, this court may dismiss the proceedings and refer the parties to arbitration or examine the validity and practicability of the arbitration agreement according to its national law. The ruling in question will not be subject to the rules of recognition and enforcement set out in Regulation (EU) n 1215/2012 Brussels I bis.

A court of a Member State may recognise and enforce or refuse to recognise and enforce an arbitral award prohibiting a party from bringing certain claims before a court of that Member State by a so-called anti-suit injunction, since

---

[25] CCJA 2nd Ch., Judgment n°03/2017 of 26th January 2017, Lexbase, n°723, 2017 obs. *Barbant A./Desplats M.*

[26] Article 14(1) UAA; ibid.

[27] Recital 12 and Article 1(2) let. d Regulation (EU) No 1215/2012; *Ménétrey S.*, L'arbitrage et le Règlement de Bruxelles I bis, p. 13–38 in: Guinchard (ed.), Le Nouveau Règlement de Bruxelles I bis, Bruylant, 2014.

[28] See Recital 12 of the Regulation; *Egéa V.*, La resolution des conflits de procedures dans le Règlement Bruxelles I bis, p. 165, in: Guinchard (ed.), Le Nouveau Règlement de Bruxelles I bis, 2014.

Brussels I bis does not govern the recognition and enforcement of an arbitral award issued by an arbitral tribunal in another Member State[29].

However, if the court considers the arbitration agreement as null and void, inoperative or incapable of being performed and decides on the substance of the matter, this should not preclude that court's judgment from being recognised or enforced in accordance with the Brussels I bis Regulation[30]. A seized court of a Member State may also ignore an anti-suit injunction of an arbitral tribunal in another Member State due to the general principle that every court itself determines, under the applicable rules of the Regulation, whether it has jurisdiction to resolve the dispute before it[31].

It should be noted, however, that this exclusion is not definitive, as certain standards of secondary European Union law appear to offer limited room for maneuver in international arbitration. This is the case with Regulation (EC) No. 1/2003 of 16 December 2002 on the implementation of competition rules.

bb) Council Regulation (EC) n° 1/2003 of 16th December 2002 on the Implementation of the Rules on Competition

This regulation empowers arbitrators and judges to apply the provisions of Article 81(1) TFEU on the regulation of the EU internal market. However, arbitration cannot result in a party being ordered to pay damages for a breach of competition law[32].

According to Article 267 of the TFEU and a judgment of 27th January 2005[33], the arbitrator may not refer questions to the CJEU for a preliminary ruling.

European public policy: The European public policy has a dual function. The first is traditional. It limits the exercise of party autonomy and the usual operation of conflict of laws rules. The second function is to apply the principle of the primacy and useful effect of European law. But the conditions for its application are not the same in all member states. In the Eco-Swiss case[34], the French court

---

[29] See on the previous regulation (EC) No 44/2001 ECJ of 13th May 2015, case C-536/13, Gazprom, n. 44; *Gascon-Inchausti F.*, La reconnaissance et l'exécution des décisions dans le Règlement Bruxelles I bis, p. 205–248, in: Guinchard (ed.), Le Nouveau Règlement de Bruxelles I bis, 2014.

[30] See Recital 12 of the Regulation; ibid.

[31] See on the previous regulation (EC) No 44/2001 ECJ of 13th May 2015, case C-536/13, Gazprom, n. 33 et seq.; ibid.

[32] Recital 7 of the Rules; Op. cit, note n°27.

[33] ECJ, case C-125/04, 27 January 2005, Guy Denuit and Betty Cordenier v Transorient – Mosaïque Voyages et Culture SA; ibid.

[34] ECJ, case C-126/97, 1 June 1999, Eco Swiss China Time Ltd v Benetton International NV; Synthèse de la table Ronde intitulée Arbitrage et droit de l'Union Européenne: Un dialogue constructif ou une collusion inévitable?, Sciences Po Paris, 27 May 2012, p. 1–11. La table ronde a été organisée par Prof. D. F. Arroyo.

refused to review the arbitration award[35], unlike the Dutch court[36], which is empowered to do so under Dutch law. In Belgium, the courts are empowered to review the arbitrators' interpretation of European law[37].

Intervention of the interim relief judge: The order of the interim relief judge can be enforced in all EU Member States on the basis of Regulation (EC) n° 805/2004 (European Enforcement Order) on one condition: The seat of the arbitral tribunal must be located within the EU Area.

Control of anti-competitive commitments: The EU Commission is responsible for investigating company mergers where the turnover of the merging companies exceeds a threshold set by EU legislation (cf. Council Regulation (EC) n°139/2004 of 20th January 2004 on the control of concentrations between undertakings).

In 2020, on the other hand, the EU Commission authorised the acquisition of Bombardier by Alstom, subject to the implementation of asset disposals. To preserve the European single market, the parties are obliged to include an arbitration clause in this type of contract, which allows the EU Commission to intervene as Amicus Curiae in arbitration proceedings. The first consequence which results from this: The secrecy of the arbitration procedure is called into question. Arbitrators are required to inform the Commission of any difficulties in interpreting the commitments. The Commission's opinion is mandatory in such cases. As a second consequence, the independence of the arbitrators is called into question.

Most EU secondary legislation excludes arbitration from its scope. In addition, arbitral awards intended to circulate within the European area are subject to the rules of European public policy. In the rare cases where arbitration is authorised by Community law (for example in the case of anti-competitive control), it is subject to conditions that call into question the normal rules governing arbitration proceedings.

2. *Mediation in Commercial Matters in OHADA and EU*

a) Mediation in Commercial Matters in OHADA

When we deal with alternative dispute resolution in commercial matters, we must also take mediation into account. The applicable legal framework within the area of the OHADA is the OHADA Uniform Act on Mediation of 23rd November 2017.

---

35 Paris Court of Appeal of 23rd March 2006 case no. 04/1967.

36 *Morbach R.*, Der kartellrechtliche ordre public in der internationalen Schiedsgerichtsbarkeit, 2021, p. 1–423.

37 Brussels Court of First Instance, Poland v Manchester Securities Corp., 18 February 2022, and Court of Cassation, 24 April 2023, Emek *İnşaat Şti* and WTE Wassertechnik v European Commission (C.21.0548.F/1), Liedekerke, 2023, obs. *Nuyts A./Hardy B.*, p. 36–38.

Scope: The Uniform Act on Mediation applies to conventional mediation in civil and commercial matters[38]. To trigger the mediation process, a mediation clause or agreement is required. This may be written or verbal[39]. The parties may opt for ad hoc or institutional mediation[40]. The parties may also have recourse to mediation in the context of arbitration or court proceedings[41].

Appointment of mediators: The parties are free to choose their mediators, whether in institutional or ad hoc mediation. The parties may call upon an authority authorised in one of the OHADA member states to appoint mediators[42]. The mediator's obligations are impartiality and independence[43], as well as to conduct the mediation diligently, to treat each party fairly and to respect their wishes[44].

Ending of mediation: The parties may decide to terminate mediation in the absence of an agreement[45]. One of the parties may unilaterally terminate the mediation process by means of a letter[46]. A partial settlement recorded in a written agreement between the parties may be grounds for terminating the mediation[47]. The mediator may also terminate the mediation in writing to the parties[48]. If an agreement is reached on all the issues dealt within mediation, the mediation process can be terminated. The agreement may be drafted by the partie's lawyers or with the help of the mediator. The content of the agreement must comply with the rules of public order[49].

Enforcement: The parties may homologate or enforce the mediation agreement in accordance with the national law of each member state. In the OHADA area, there is no regional mediation centre as there is for arbitration. However,

[38] Articles 1 and 2 Uniform Act on Mediation (UAM); *Sossa D. C./Tchakoua J.-M./ Agbenoto K. M.*, Droit de la mediation, 2023, p. 35–36.

[39] Article 4 UAM; *Dingle J./Kelbie J.*, The Mediation Handbook 2013–2014, London school of Mediation Limited, 2013, p. 14; *Ben Yaich M.*, La médiation contractuelle: lecture dans le texte juridique, Revista de Estudios Fronterizos del Estrecho de Gibraltar, n°3 2016, p. 1–10.

[40] Article 1(3) UAM; *Bühler M. W./Gidoin A.-S.*, Le point sur le 10èm Acte Uniforme de l'OHADA sur la médiation, Lexbase *n°749*, 2018, p. 1–11.

[41] Article 4(3) UAM; ibid., note 38, p. 17 et seq.; *Cadiet L.*, La médiation, une justice sans juge?, *BDE*, n°2, 2017, p. 7.

[42] Article 5(2) UAM; ibid., note 38, p. 48.

[43] Article 6 UAM; *Otis L./Rousseau-Saine C.*, Le médiateur et les dilemmes éthiques: proposition d'un cadre de réflexion, in: M.-A. Raouf (ed.), From the Arab World to the Globalization of International Law and Arbitration, Alphen aan den Rijn, 2015, p. 124.

[44] Article 7 UAM; ibid.

[45] Article 12 UAM; note 38, p. 113 et seq.; *Brusorio Aillaud M.*, Droit des obligations, 9th ed., 2018, n°394.

[46] Article 12 UAM; note 38, p. 91 et seq.

[47] Article 12 UAM; *Cadiet L.* Le procès entre rapidité et flexibilité, in: Mélanges en l'honneur de Jacques Mestre, Liber Amicorum, 2019, p. 1–92.

[48] Article 12 UAM; ibid. note 38, p. 107–109.

[49] Article 9 UAM; *Huchet G.*, La clause de médiation, Thèse de Doctorat, Université Jean Moulin-Lyon 3, 2007, p. 341.

the application of the Uniform Act on Simplified Procedures and Means of Enforcement (AUPSVE) facilitates the enforcement of mediation agreements in the member states.

b) Mediation in commercial matters in EU area

Directive 2008/52/EC of 21st May 2008 on certain aspects of mediation in civil and commercial matters has a limited scope of application: It applies to cross-border disputes in civil and commercial matters[50]. The dispute must first of all be cross-border in nature and therefore display a foreign element[51]. Civil and commercial matters are not simply a reference to the domestic law of the Member States but are an autonomous concept[52]. Furthermore, individual disputes between two or more parties are required. Lastly, the parties must freely express their wish to resolve the dispute through mediation.

The mediation process must be structured, with guarantees of the confidentiality of the procedure[53], equal treatment of the parties in terms of information sharing, and enforceability of the mediation agreement through homologation by a national judge. The content of the mediated agreement must comply with public policy.

The scope of EU secondary legislation on mediation is limited to cross-border commercial disputes, unlike the OHADA Uniform Act on Mediation, which has a wider scope. For the enforcement of mediation agreements, there is no regional uniform law that applies in the EU area, unlike the rules in force in the OHADA area. However, each national court or authority applies its own national law.

IV. Conclusion

In OHADA law, the unification of the entire legal framework of business law at regional level has led to the unification of judicial procedures through the CCJA. The introduction of Uniform Acts regulating commercial companies, general trade and economic interest groupings, arbitration, mediation and sim-

---

50 Recital 8, Article 1(2), phr. 1 and Article 2 Directive 2008/52/EC; *Petit V. E.*, La médiation de la consommation: une procédure obligatoire pour toutes les entreprises à partir du 1er janvier 2016, D. 2015, p. 2571, spéc. n° 4; *Poli C.*, Médiation des litiges de la consommation: vers l'affirmation d'un droit au recours à la résolution amiable des différends, REDC 2015/2, spéc. p. 350.

51 Article 2(1) Directive 2008/52/EC; *Pizzio J.-P.*, Le règlement extrajudiciaire des litiges de consommation: apports des nouveaux textes européens, RLDA 2013, p. 85.

52 CJEU, Case C-420/07, 28 April 2009, Apostolides, n. 73.

53 Article 7 Directive 2008/52/EC; *Guinchard E./Boucaron-Nardetto M.*, France, in: Civil and Commercial Mediation in Europe, Volume I, 2012, p. 132–157.

plified enforcement procedures at regional level facilitates the settlement of commercial disputes by the courts and by alternative means, namely arbitration and mediation.

The EU could draw inspiration from OHADA's legal and judicial practice. It could, for example, encourage the introduction of a European Business Code to harmonise business law in the EU area in order to make the business environment more attractive.

On the other hand, OHADA law may be inspired by the European Enforcement Order mechanism to better coordinate in the Member States the harmonisation of the enforcement of arbitration awards that have benefited from the exequatur of the CCJA judge.

Practical Experiences on Implementing OHADA and EU Law

Jean Jacques Lecat

I. Introduction

In Africa like in Europe, businesses are increasingly expanding beyond national borders through various means, including direct investments, acquisitions in multiple countries, and mergers involving companies from different States. This article aims to analyse the respective effects of European Union (EU) regulations and business law enacted by the Organization for the Harmonization of Business Law in Africa (OHADA)[1], which is frequently presented as a benchmark model for legal unification within a regional area, in the context of the implementation of transnational investment projects in the Member States of these two organizations. This analysis is based on a comparative examination of four specific areas: Company law (I), access to information on commercial companies (II), accounting rules (III), and tax treatment of cross border financial flows (IV). Before addressing these aspects, it is necessary to highlight the fundamental differences between the EU and OHADA, both in terms of their general objectives and the legal instruments used to achieve them.

1. EU and OHADA Distinct Objectives and Scopes

The overarching objectives and institutional frameworks of the EU and OHADA differ significantly.

The EU operates as a supranational political and economic union with a broad mandate that includes, in particular, the creation of a single internal market, the promotion of social and territorial cohesion, environmental sustainability, and political goals related to peace and stability, promotion of democracy and strengthening the EU's global influence. Within the broader EU objectives, the right to establish and manage enterprises, including cross-border corporate

[1] The Treaty establishing the Organization for the Harmonization of Business Law in Africa (OHADA) was signed on 17th October 1993, in Port Louis (Mauritius) and revised in Quebec City (Canada) on 17th October 2008. The current 17 Member States to the OHADA Treaty are: Benin, Burkina Faso, Comoros, Mali, Niger, Central African Republic, Sénégal (1995), Cameroon, Côte d'Ivoire, Guinea Bissau, Tchad, Togo (1996), Gabon (1998), Republic of Congo, Equatorial Guinea (1999), Republic of Guinea (2000), Democratic Republic of Congo (2012).

groups, is inherent to the freedom of establishment, and more generally, is part of the completion of the internal market[2].

The Treaty on the Functioning of the European Union (TFEU) delineates the distribution of competences between the Union and its Member States, distinguishing between areas of exclusive Union competence and those of shared competence. In domains of shared competence, such as the internal market, Member States may legislate and adopt legally binding acts only to the extent that the Union has not exercised its competence[3].

In contrast, OHADA is a regional legal integration initiative focused specifically on the unification and modernization of business law across its Member States, rather than the establishment of a single market, to which the OHADA Treaty makes no reference[4]. The OHADA Treaty provides, without limitation, examples of areas falling within the scope of business law[5]. The Council of Ministers, OHADA's legislative body, may unanimously decide to include new matters in the OHADA corpus of business laws.

However, several OHADA Members States also participate in other African regional organizations – such as the West African Economic and Monetary Union (WAEMU)[6], the Central African Economic and Monetary Community (CEMAC)[7] and the Economic Community of West African States (ECOW-

---

[2] According to Article 49(1) TFEU restrictions of the freedom of establishment of nationals of a Member State in the territory of another Member State including restrictions on the setting-up of agencies, branches or subsidiaries by nationals of any Member State established in the territory of any Member State is prohibited, and Article 49(2) guarantees to set up and manage undertakings, in particular companies or firms.

[3] Article 2(2) and Article 4(2)(a) TFEU.

[4] The purpose of the OHADA Treaty is specifically to "harmonize business law in the States Parties by the elaboration and adoption of simple modern common rules adapted to their economies and by setting up appropriate judicial procedures and promoting arbitration as a means of settling contractual disputes" (Article 1 of the OHADA Treaty).

[5] According to Article 2 of the Treaty: "For the purposes of this Treaty, the field of business law shall include all rules all regulations concerning company laws and the legal status of merchants, debt recovery, security interests and enforcing proceedings, companies receivership and judicial liquidation, arbitration law, labour law, accounting law, transportation and sale of goods laws and any other matter that the Council of Ministers may unanimously decide to include [...]".

[6] The West African Economic and Monetary Union (WAEMU) was created as a monetary union by the Treaty dated 14th November 1973, last amended on 20th January 2007, supplemented by the Treaty establishing the West African Economic and Monetary Union of 10th January 1994, amended on 29th January 2003. WAEMU comprises eight States: Benin, Burkina Faso, Côte d'Ivoire, Guinea-Bissau, Mali, Niger, Senegal, and Togo, all of which are also members of OHADA. The Republic of Guinea, which is an OHADA Member, is not a member of WAEMU.

[7] The Central African Economic and Monetary Community (CEMAC) has been established by a Treaty of 16th March 1994, revised on 30th January 2009. CEMAC comprises six states: Cameroon, the Central African Republic, the Republic of the Congo, Gabon, Equatorial Guinea, and Chad, all of which are also members of OHADA. In accordance with the Treaty, the Member States of CEMAC established two unions in accordance with two con-

AS)[8] – which pursue objectives more closely aligned with those of the European Union, including the creation of a customs union, a single market, and an economic and monetary union[9]. The overlapping membership of states in OHADA and in these economically integrative organizations raises the potential for conflicts of norms.

2. EU and OHADA Legal Instruments

The nature and scope of legislative instruments necessary to implement their objectives differ significantly between the European Union and OHADA.

a) EU Legal Instruments

To ensure the establishment and functioning of the internal market, including the freedom of establishment, the European Parliament and the Council adopt measures aiming at the approximation of national laws and regulations of Member States that impact the internal market[10]. EU institutions utilize to this end various legal instruments, notably Regulations – directly applicable and binding in full – and Directives, which bind Member States as to the result but require national transposition.

Directives are especially prevalent in areas marked by divergent legal traditions, such as the matters related to regulations relating to the freedom of establishment and the legal framework for the development of groups of companies. EU action must also be guided by the principles of subsidiarity and proportionality, as set forth in Article 5 of the Treaty on European Union. Subsidiarity limits Union intervention in areas not falling within the Union's exclusive competence to cases where objectives cannot be effectively achieved by Member States alone, while proportionality ensures that EU measures do not exceed what is necessary.

ventions: the Convention of the Economic Union of Central Africa governing the Economic Union of Central Africa (EUC) of 16th July 1996, and the Convention of the Monetary Union of Central Africa (MUCA) of 5th July 1996, both revised on 25th June 2008.

[8] The ECOWAS Treaty was signed on 28th May 1975 by fifteen countries. After the withdrawal of Burkina Faso, Mali and Niger on 29th January 2025, the current thirteen Member States of ECOWAS are: Benin, Cabo Verde, Côte d'Ivoire, The Gambia, Ghana, Guinea, Guinea Bissau, Liberia, Nigeria, Sierra Leone, Sénégal and Togo.

[9] Each of these regional organizations also contemplated the establishment of a common currency among its Member States. However, to date, only WAEMU and CEMAC have implemented this objective. Within both unions, a single currency – the CFA franc – is utilized, maintained at a fixed exchange rate with the euro and managed under the authority of two distinct central banks. It is important to note that, despite sharing the same currency name and parity, the two monetary zones operate independently and are institutionally separate.

[10] As provided under Articles 26, 114, and 115 TFEU.

National authorities are given some flexibility in transposing Directives into their national legal system. However, they must comply with certain procedural rules regarding the communication to the European Commission of the measures that they intend to use in order to achieve the transposition. In addition, the transposition of Directives must take place by the deadline set when the Directive is adopted and the Commission may initiate infringement proceedings against the Member State before the Court of Justice of the European Union, if it does not transpose a Directive.

b) OHADA Uniform Acts

Within the OHADA, the system of common rules of business law is achieved by means of Uniform Acts, which are the only type of instrument[11]. Uniform Acts are directly applicable in Member States ninety days after their publication in the OHADA Official Journal, without any national ratification or publication formalities or procedures, and repeal all contrary or identical provisions of national laws, having the same subject matter, whether prior or subsequent.

Member States need only intervene in a few cases where the Uniform Acts require implementing legislation at the national level, for instance in order to determine the sanctions applicable to criminal offenses defined by Uniform Acts or to implement the digitization of the business register or to determine the supporting judge competent to take decisions in arbitration proceedings. In this regard, no deadline has been set for states to adopt these implementing measures, and no penalties are provided for failure to do so.

Eleven Uniform Acts are currently in force, which cover the main area of business law[12]. The Uniform Acts establish a system of identical laws in the

[11] Uniform Acts are adopted by the Council of Ministers composed of the Minister of Justice and the Minister of Finance of each State. They have a single vote on behalf of the State they represent. The Council of Ministers may only deliberate if at least two-thirds of the States Parties are represented. It determines the matters that may be subject to harmonization and adopts Uniform Acts by unanimous vote of the States Parties present and voting, each State having one vote.

[12] Uniform Acts currently in force include: Uniform Act on General Commercial Law (first enacted in 1997, revised in 2010); Uniform Act on Commercial Companies and the Economic Interest Groupings (first enacted in 1997, revised in 2014); Uniform Act on Security Interests (first enacted in 1997, revised in 2010); Uniform Act on the Organization of Collective Procedures for the Discharge of Liabilities (first enacted in 1998, revised in 2015); Uniform Act on Arbitration (first enacted in 1998, revised in 2017); Uniform Act on Mediation (Adopted 2017); Uniform Act on Accounting Law and Financial Reporting (AUDCIF) (first enacted in 2000, revised in 2017); Uniform Act on the Organization and Harmonization of Accounting for Non-Profit Entities (Adopted 2022); Uniform Act on Cooperatives (Adopted 2010); Uniform Act on Contracts for the Carriage of Goods by Road (Adopted 2003); Uniform Act Organizing Simplified Recovery Procedures and Enforcement Measures (first enacted in 2000, revised in 2023).

seventeen Member States, creating a legal framework ensuring legal certainty conducive to investment and facilitating cross-border trade and investment.

II. Company Law

When acquiring or developing a group of companies in several states, the diversity of rules applicable to the creation and operation of commercial companies constitutes a major obstacle.

1. Limits of Harmonized Company Law within EU

The main purpose of EU rules is to enable businesses to be set up anywhere in the EU without restrictions. In addition, to relieve restrictions, these rules, without codifying company law, have established minimum standards related to companies, to be implemented by Member States, now consolidated by Directive (EU) 2017/1132 of the European Parliament and of the Council of 14th June 2017 relating to certain aspects of company law (a), and a European form of company, the European Company (Societas Europaea or SE), has been instituted under Regulation (EC) No 2157/2001 (b).

a) Companies' Standards and Guidelines

Directive (EU) 2017/1132 consolidates and codifies various earlier Directives relating to company law. It establishes, among other provisions, a minimum capital requirement for public limited liability companies to serve as a safeguard for creditors requiring a counterpart to the limited liability enjoyed by shareholders. The Directive also provides guidelines for a legal framework for single-member private limited liability companies, aiming at facilitating entrepreneurship and corporate flexibility across Member States. In addition, Directive 2017/1132 sets out minimum standards for the regulation of takeover bids and changes of control, with the objective of protecting minority shareholders, employees, and other interested parties. It also introduces provisions for the interconnection of national business registers (see paragraph III.1). The rules for cross-border conversions, mergers and divisions, set forth by Directive 2017/1132 have been amended by Directive (EU) 2019/2121 of the Parliament and the Council of 27th November 2019[13].

---

[13] The changes introduced by this Directive include in particular: harmonized uniform rules for cross-border conversions and divisions, which were not previously regulated at the EU level, and alignment of rules governing cross-border mergers, with new rules on cross-border conversions and divisions; establishing a common multi-layer procedure governing cross-border divisions by formation of new companies; a simplified merger procedure for "less complex mergers".

These minimum standards and guidelines prevent national laws from providing rules that are contrary to the principles laid down in the Treaties and introduce a certain degree of harmonization. They do not, however, succeed in establishing the legal certainty and predictability of uniform rules, eliminating discrepancies between national laws of Member States, which would allow the creation of Europe-wide companies implied by the development of the internal market. They leave a diversity of company forms that appears, in particular, in the lists of limited liability company forms existing in the EU Member States, as set out in the Annexes to the Directives above mentioned.

b) European Company (Societas Europaea or SE)

The European Company form, established by Regulation (EC) No 2157/2001, is designed to facilitate cross-border business within the EU by allowing companies to operate under a single European legal structure and to facilitate the creation of groups of companies from different Member States[14].

However, the conditions set forth for its creation and operation limit the possibilities of using it. An SE can only be formed with a minimum capital of EUR 120,000 and under the following conditions:
(i) By Merger: Two or more public limited-liability companies from different EU Member States can merge to form an SE.
(ii) As a Holding SE: Public or private limited-liability companies from different Member States, or having had cross-border subsidiaries or branches for at least two years, can form a holding in SE form.
(iii) As a Subsidiary SE: Companies or legal entities from different Member States, or having had cross-border operations for at least two years, can jointly form a subsidiary SE.
(iv) By Transformation: A public limited-liability company having had a cross-border subsidiary for at least two years can convert into an SE.

In addition, some key governance aspects of the SE must be determined by the national company law of the Member State where the SE is registered, which undermines the clarity of rules governing the SE:
- The board structure, either a supervisory organ and a management organ (two-tier system as in German and Austrian company law) or an administrative organ (one-tier system as in Swedish and Spanish company law) depending on the form adopted in the statutes (as traditionally allowed by French and Dutch company law);

---

[14] According to the recital of Regulation (EC) No 2157/2001: "the legal framework within which business must be carried on in the Community is still based largely on national laws and therefore no longer corresponds to the economic framework within which it must develop if the objectives set out in Article 18 of the Treaty are to be achieved. That situation forms a considerable obstacle to the creation of groups of companies from different Member States".

- The responsibilities, liabilities, and disqualification rules applicable to directors and the rules governing the meetings and the voting rules applicable to the adoption of shareholders' assembly resolutions, are defined by the national company law applicable in the Member State where the SE's registered office is situated;
- Directive 2001/86/EC establishes a negotiating procedure to involve the employees in the affairs of the SE. These rules supplement the national rules, which remain applicable if negotiations fail.
- If the special negotiating body decided not to open negotiations or to terminate negotiations already opened or if the period for negotiations pursuant to Article 5 of Directive 2001/86/EC has expired without an agreement on arrangements for employee involvement pursuant to Article 4 of Directive 2001/86/EC having been concluded, the national fallback provisions apply, which vary widely across Member States.

The objective set at the time of the SE's creation, to establish a uniform legal framework within which companies from different Member States could plan and carry out the restructuring of their business activities at Community level, has therefore not been achieved.

2. Companies in OHADA Member States

Commercial companies incorporated in each of the OHADA Member States are governed by the Uniform Act on Commercial Companies and Economic Interest Groupings, which constitutes the companies act of the seventeen OHADA Member States and sets out all the rules relating to their creation and operation, from which the States may not derogate, except in very rare cases[15].

The 2014 revised version of the Uniform Act on Commercial Companies and Economic Interest Groupings offers a variety of company forms, including the simplified joint stock company, which allows for considerable flexibility in governance, and contains modern provisions enabling, in particular, the establishment of investor-friendly shareholder relations, such as the possibility of creating classes of shares or bonds convertible into shares[16].

---

[15] Regarding limited liability companies Member States may adopt provisions that differ from those laid down in the Uniform Act with regard to the amount of the minimum share capital and the obligation to use a notary for its incorporation. Other exceptions relate to the application of special rules required for specific economic sectors including those governing credit institutions within the meaning of banking law, microfinance institutions and financial market participants, as well as those of insurance and reinsurance companies.

[16] Under the OHADA Uniform Act relating to Commercial Companies and Economic Interest Groupings (AUSCGIE), the following forms of commercial companies or entities are recognized: Société en Nom Collectif (SNC) – General Partnership: Partners are jointly and severally liable for the company's debts; Société en Commandite Simple (SCS) – Limited Partnership: Comprises general partners (with unlimited liability) and limited partners (liable

III. Access to Information on Commercial Companies

Having quick access to reliable information on the legal and financial status of companies is essential, in particular in the context of the development of multinational groups within unions such as the EU and OHADA and for the protection of creditors. This information is generally provided by business registers. In the context of the development of multinational groups within unions such as the EU and OHADA, it is necessary to have access to information from the registers of all Member States.

1. EU Business Registers Interconnection System (BRIS)

Business registers of all EU Member States and of two EEA countries are connected to the Business Registers Interconnection System (BRIS), established by Directive 2012/17/EU of the European Parliament and of the Council of 13th June 2012 (the "BRIS Directive"), which became operational in June 2017. The scope of BRIS and technical specifications and procedures required for an effective and secure interconnection system of the business registers have been set out in various Directives and implementing Regulations.

BRIS offers two main functions: (i) cross-border access to information related to limited liability companies incorporated within the EU and on branches of these companies and (ii) exchange of information between business registers[17]:

(i) The public can access information on EU limited liability companies and on branches of these companies incorporated within the EU through the "search for a company in the EU" page of the European e-Justice Portal. Basic information accessible free of charge includes the name and legal form of the company, the registered office, the Member State of registration and the registration number. Company documents made available by the national business registers may also be obtained through BRIS. The portal also gives access to the national business register of the Member States;

---

only up to their contributions); Société à Responsabilité Limitée (SARL) – Private Limited Liability Company: Liability of members is limited to their contributions. Common among small and medium-sized enterprises; Société Anonyme (SA) – Public Limited Company: Suitable for large businesses, with shareholders' liability limited to their contributions. Requires a minimum share capital and a board of directors or a general director and supervisory board; Société en Commandite par Actions (SCA) – Partnership Limited by Shares: A hybrid of a partnership and a corporation, with both general partners and shareholders; Société Coopérative (SC) – Cooperative.

17 Directive (EU) 2017/1132 of the European Parliament and of the Council, amended by Directive (EU) 2019/1151 of the European Parliament and of the Council of 20th June 2019 lays down inter alia rules on disclosure and interconnection of central, commercial and companies registers of Member States.

(ii) The exchange of information among business registers on cross-border issues in view of improving their accuracy and reliability, includes information on the opening and termination of winding-up or insolvency proceedings, on mergers between companies registered in different Member States (allowing for the deletion of the registration of the companies that have ceased to exist as a result of the merger) and more recently on disqualified directors, ensuring that any application to register a person for an executive position that he or she is banned from exercising, in accordance with the relevant laws of the EU Member State where the company is incorporated, is refused, and that this information is exchanged with business registers of other EU Member States[18].

In addition, harmonized procedures for cross-border conversion allowing a company to change its legal form and move its registered office to another Member State, while retaining its legal personality, and divisions of a company by formation of new companies have been established including protection mechanisms for employees, creditors and minority shareholders.

BRIS does not aim at harmonizing national systems of commercial and companies registers and does not provide for any obligation on the Member States to change their internal systems of registers. Member States retain a margin of discretion in the transposition of Directive (EU) 2017/1132, particularly with respect to procedural and technical modalities. Nevertheless, they are under a binding obligation to ensure full implementation of the Directive's harmonized substantive provisions, notably those pertaining to transparency, legal certainty, and cross-border cooperation, in accordance with the principles of EU law.

The Commission has also developed an electronic interconnection of Member States insolvency registers, available on the European e-Justice Portal as part of BRIS, which had to be set up by 2018 in accordance with EU Regulation on insolvency proceedings[19]. This system is a service interconnecting and giving access to the existing decentralized national insolvency registers of the Member States and does not constitute a centralized EU insolvency register. According to the information provided by the European e-Justice Portal not all EU Member States are fully connected to the centralized insolvency and bankruptcy register search system and the level of information varies depending on the country. The registers record, analyse and store insolvency information and make it available to the public, albeit in various forms, depending on the country.

---

[18] Digitalisation Directive (Directive 2019/1151) and Mobility Directive (Directive 2019/2121).

[19] Regulation on insolvency proceedings 2015/848 of the European Parliament and of the Council of 20th May 2015.

Some countries have a dedicated register and publish information on all stages of the insolvency proceedings and on the parties to the proceedings, and others only publish the name and the status of a company. Certain countries use other registers (such as Commercial registers or Court registers).

It is also worth noting that Regulation 2015/848 mainly deals with conflict of laws in case of international insolvency proceedings while the type and the course of insolvency proceedings provided by domestic law remains largely national with significant differences, which makes it difficult to appraise the information provided[20].

2. *OHADA Registre du Commerce et du Crédit Mobilier – RCCM*

The rules governing business registers (Registre du Commerce et du Crédit Mobilier – RCCM – Commercial and Security Interests Register) in OHADA Member States are included in the Uniform Act on General Commercial Law.

In all Member States Business Registers must include data on:

- Registration, creation, amendments and termination of activity of natural persons and of all forms of companies carrying out business activities;
- Conclusion, renewal and termination of equipment leasing agreements and security interests governed by the Uniform Act on Security Interests;
- Court decisions related to insolvency proceedings made in accordance with the Uniform Act on the organization of collective debt settlement procedures, to be forwarded by relevant courts;
- Court decisions related to financial or assets penalties against company executives;
- Annual financial statements and minutes of board and general assembly meetings must also be forwarded to the Registers.

A register is kept at the level of each local court and a National Register compiles data from all local registers in each Member State. In addition, a Regional Register held at the OHADA Common Court of Justice and Arbitration centralizes all information forwarded by National Registers.

Model forms to be used by registers of all OHADA Member States are established and disseminated by the OHADA organization. Provisions in view of receiving, keeping and disseminating data by electronic means have been intro-

---

[20] Regulation 2015/848 harmonizes the following key subjects across EU Member States: rules for determining which Member State's courts have jurisdiction to open insolvency proceedings, based on the debtor's "center of main interests" (COMI); automatic recognition of insolvency proceedings and related judgments across Member States, without the need for further formalities, national law applicable to insolvency proceedings, generally the law of the Member State where proceedings are opened, allowing for the initiation of secondary proceedings in another Member State where the debtor has an establishment in view of local creditors protection.

duced by the 2010 Uniform Act on General Commercial Law repelling and replacing the previous Act.

Thanks to the uniform laws governing business registers, company information, insolvency proceedings, and security interests across all Member States, the information contained in the commercial register refers to identical concepts in all Member States. However, access to the information that these registers are meant to provide has been hindered in particular by incomplete data transmission and delays in the digitalization of registers by OHADA Member States. Progress in computerizing these registers accelerated once the OHADA central organization acquired dedicated software and funded both its deployment and the necessary equipment in the Member States.

IV. Accounting Rules

In order to promote multi-country investments within regional organizations like the EU and OHADA and international commercial transactions, it is not sufficient that the information provided in accounting statements gives a true and fair view of the assets, financial position, and results of a business. This information must also be equivalent, regardless of the country in which a company is established.

1. EU Common Accounting Rules

Accounting rules are different for listed companies in an EU-regulated market and for unlisted companies.

EU Regulations provide for International Financial Reporting Standards (IFRS) to be used by all listed companies in an EU-regulated market for preparing their consolidated financial statements[21]. The Commission, assisted by an accounting regulatory committee, decide on the applicability of the modifications to IFRS or of new standards issued or adopted by the International Accounting Standards Board (IASB). The use of IFRS for individual financial statements of listed companies and for consolidated or individual accounts of non-listed companies is decided by Member States.

Most EU countries permit IFRS for consolidated accounts of non-listed companies (however, Czech Republic, Hungary and Poland are examples of countries where IFRS are used only by listed companies and national rules are used

[21] As provided for by Regulation (EC) No 1606/2002 of the European Parliament and of the Council of 19th July 2002 and Commission Regulation (EU) No 2023/1803 of 13th August 2023 adopting certain international accounting standards in accordance with Regulation (EC) No 1606/2002 of the European Parliament and of the Council, consolidating all IFRS and related interpretations adopted by the EU up to 8th September 2022.

by non-listed companies). Few countries allow IFRS for individual accounts of non-listed companies (e.g.: Ireland, Netherland) while in others national rules apply.

When the use of IFRS is not mandatory, non-listed companies must comply with national accounting standards, which must follow the rules set by Directive 2013/34/EU (the "Accounting Directive"), adopted with reference to the freedom of establishment.

The Accounting Directive defines the criteria for classifying assets and liabilities as well as income and expenses of companies, sets out the rules for establishing the annual financial statements and related reports and provides an overall layout of the balance sheet and of the profit and loss account. A part of these rules apply unless national law provides otherwise. It also simplifies the financial reporting requirements for micro-enterprises in order to enhance their competitiveness and introduces an obligation for EU listed companies to provide a corporate governance statement in their annual report.

In view of improving the reliability of companies' financial statements another Directive defines the role, responsibilities and minimum requirements of statutory auditors and audit firms.

The EU accounting rules applicable to unlisted companies aim to ensure the comparability and equivalence of financial information by stating minimum common standards. They do not endeavour to achieve complete harmonization of accounting rules.

2. *OHADA Accounting System*

Accounting law is mentioned in Article 2 of the OHADA Treaty among the examples of business law matters. A first Uniform Act on Accounting Law was enacted on 24th March 2000. However accounting standards were already adopted by WAEMU in 1996, which created a conflict of norms in countries which were members of both organizations[22].

This conflict was solved by the enactment by WAEMU of a Regulation harmonizing its West African Accounting System (SYSCOA) with the OHADA Uniform Act on Accounting. Both accounting systems coexisted but were identical.

A new conflict emerged in 2013 when WAEMU revised the SYSCOA, resulting in a misalignment with the OHADA Uniform Act on Accounting Law.

On this matter, the Conference of Heads of State and Government of OHADA Member States – which includes all WAEMU member countries and serves as OHADA's highest authority – mandated, during its session on 17th October 2013, that the OHADA Council of Ministers continue the revision of the Uni-

22 See supra I 1.

form Act on Accounting Law. It was also agreed that this revised Act would constitute the sole set of accounting standards applicable in all OHADA Member States, including those that are also members of WAEMU.

On the basis of this decision, a new Uniform Act on Accounting Law and Financial Reporting (UAAFR) was adopted on 26th January 2017, which became the sole accounting reference for all OHADA Member States, including a new chart of accounts (SYSCOHADA).

In addition to setting the rules for qualifying financial transactions and for establishing financial statements, the SYSCOHADA chart of accounts provides a detailed list of accounts to be used when recording transactions. An application guide was also prepared which includes accounting entries for the transactions. As a result, companies' activities are recorded uniformly, and their financial statements are prepared according to the same standardized procedures across all OHADA Member States.

V. Tax Treatment of Cross Border Financial Flows

Reducing and harmonizing taxes on financial flows between companies based in different countries is a key factor in fostering the growth of multinational groups. Under national laws dividends, interest, and royalties paid across borders are subject to withholding taxes. While bilateral tax treaties often lower these rates, they rarely eliminate them entirely. In the absence of specific tax provisions – particularly regarding the treatment of received dividends – an additional tax burden may arise when the receiving company is also subject to corporate income tax on those earnings.

This issue is addressed within the European Union through its common system of taxation. OHADA does not legislate on tax matters. However, the majority of OHADA Member States also belong to other regional organizations that establish rules to prevent double taxation.

1. EU Common System of Taxation

Although direct taxation falls outside the European Union's core competencies, several Directives have been adopted to establish a common system of taxation of dividends, interests and royalties paid between affiliated companies. These measures have been adopted to facilitate the integration of companies from different Member States, thereby supporting the creation of a single EU market with the characteristics of a domestic market and ensuring its effective operation.

Recognizing that tax rules governing cross-border corporate relationships varied significantly among Member States – and were generally less favourable than those applied to domestic corporate relations –, the EU identified a need to eliminate such disparities, considering that addressing these distortions was essential to promote cross-border cooperation and group formation under conditions comparable to those within a single national market.

Since these disparities directly impacted the establishment and functioning of the internal market and could not be adequately addressed by individual Member States, the Council adopted the Directives on the common system of taxation under Article 115 TFEU, in line with the principle of subsidiarity.

These Directives introduced a common tax framework, initially covering dividends and profit distributions from subsidiaries to parent companies across Member States and later extending to interest and royalty payments between associated companies established in different Member States.

The common system of taxation applicable to dividends between a subsidiary and its parent company provided the parent company holds at least 10 % in the capital of its subsidiary, provides for:

- The exemption from withholding tax of dividends and other profit distributions paid by subsidiary companies of a Member State to their parent companies established in another Member State;
- The exemption of dividends received by the parent company from corporate income tax or, if they are taxed, by granting a deduction from the amount of tax due of that fraction of the corporation tax related to the profits distributed by the subsidiary and any lower-tier subsidiary.

The common system of taxation applicable to interest and royalty payments, set up by Council Directive 2003/49/EC of 3rd June 2003, aims at avoiding double taxation by exempting interests and royalties paid by a company of a Member State to an associated company of another Member State from any withholding tax. If a tax is wrongly withheld by the Member State from which interests or royalties are paid, this Member State must refund it within one year, with interest due if the refund is delayed.

Two companies are regarded as associated under the Interest and Royalties Directive when one has a direct minimum holding of 25 % in the capital of the other, or when a third company has a direct minimum holding of 25 % in the capital of both companies.

In order to benefit from the common tax regime provided for in both Directives:

- The companies concerned must take one of the forms of limited liability companies listed in the Annexes to the Directives and be subject to corporate income tax.
- The recipient of the dividends, interests or royalties must be the beneficial owner of the payment.

The accuracy of these measures has enabled them to be transposed precisely into national legislation and to effectively facilitate financial flows between affiliated companies within the Union.

2. *Tax Treatment of Financial Flows within OHADA*

Withholding tax rates applied by OHADA Member States national tax legislation on dividends, interests and royalties are generally high and vary significantly from State to State.

Tax law is not considered part of the business law that OHADA aims to uniformize.

Measures to avoid double taxation are taken within the framework of other organizations of which OHADA Member States are also members, based on the idea of a single market, which is their main objective. CEMAC, WAEMU and ECOWAS Member States have respectively adopted rules on the avoidance of double taxation[23].

Regarding dividends, interests and royalties these measures are geared towards limiting the rate of applicable withholding taxes and granting a tax credit to the beneficiary company as generally provided for by non-double taxation. The maximum tax rates are shown in *table 1*.

Table 1

Type of payment	Maximum applicable rates		
	Between ECOWAS Member States	Between WAEMU Member States	Between CEMAC Member States
Dividends	10 %	10 %	5 % to parent company holding at least 25 % of the subsidiary's capital 10 % in other cases
Interests	10 %	15 %	10 %
Royalties	10 %	15 %	10 %

Since these measures apply only between Member States of the respective regional organizations, financial flows between companies of two OHADA

[23] Règlement n°08/2008/CM/UEMOA portant non-double imposition des entreprises communautaires adopted on 26th June 2008; Supplementary Act A/S A6 12/18 adopting community rules for the elimination of double taxation with respect to taxes on income, capital and inheritance and the prevention of tax evasion and avoidance within the ECOWAS Member States, dated 22nd December 2018; Règlement n°07/19-UEAC-0103-cm-33 portant révision de l'Acte n°5/66-UDEAC-49 du 13 Décembre 1966 relatif à la Convention sur la non double imposition à l'IRPP.

Member States that do not both belong to one of these organizations do not benefit from any provisions aimed at reducing the tax burden on such transactions.

For instance, financial flows between companies registered in Côte d'Ivoire, a member of WAEMU and ECOWAS, and companies registered in Cameroon, member of CEMAC, the two largest economies among OHADA Member States, do not benefit from any measures limiting double taxation on financial flows. As a consequence, dividends, interests and royalties are subject to the withholding taxes shown in *table 2*. These taxes apply with no limitations and do not give rise to any tax credit.

Table 2

Nature of payment	Withholding tax on gross amount	
	On payment from Côte d'Ivoire	On payment from Cameroun
Dividends	17 %	16,5 %
Interests	18 %	16,5 %
Royalties	20 %	15 %

VI. Conclusion

Neither the harmonization efforts of the European Union nor the unification approach of OHADA fully meet expectations.

In the EU, harmonization in business law is primarily driven by the economic objectives of the Treaties and still allows for significant divergences between national legal systems in key areas of business law. This fragmentation results in legal uncertainty, increased compliance and administrative costs, and ultimately acts as a barrier to cross-border investment. These challenges have given rise to discussions regarding a unified European Business Law Code encompassing areas such as commercial law, corporate law, insolvency, banking, insurance, intellectual property, labour, taxation[24].

OHADA, as a specialized legal integration organization, faces competition from broader regional organizations with wider mandates. To expand its influence, OHADA could consider entering into agreements with these organizations to harmonize their respective legal frameworks within their areas of competence. Another potential avenue is the geographical expansion of OHADA's

[24] See for instance: *Enrico Letta* (Institut Jacques Delors), Much More Than a Market, report presented to the European Council on 18th April 2024; *Philippe Dupichot*, Designing a common European business law, Revue Européenne du Droit 2021/2 no. 3, 108–113.

membership. This implies that candidate countries must adopt all OHADA uniform instruments in their entirety, without exception, thereby repealing any conflicting national provisions on the same subjects, which may constitute an obstacle.

List of authors

Prof. Dr. Gérard Ngoumtsa Anou
Professor of Private Law, University of Grenoble

Paul Bayzelon
Member of the Board of Directors, Groupe Loret, Paris, and Secretary of the Association pour l'Unification du Droit en Afrique (UNIDA)

Prof. Dr. Peter Jung, Maître en droit
Professor of Private Law, University of Basel

Dr. Nestor Kouami
Attorney at the Paris Bar; Postdoc at the World Trade Institute of the University of Bern; Head of the Arbitration Unit of the Youth Section of the African Academy of International Law Practice

Jean Jacques Lecat
Attorney at the Paris Bar, Chairman of the Law and Tax Committee of the French Council of Investors in Africa

Univ.-Prof. Dr. Matthias Lehmann
Professor of Private Law, Private International Law, and Comparative Law, University of Vienna

Dr. Seyoum Yohannes Tesfay
Legal and Economic Consultant, Berlin

Index